Art Quilts
Playing with a full deck

SUE PIERCE AND

VERNA SUIT

POMEGRANATE ARTBOOKS ♠ ♥ ♦ ♣ SAN FRANCISCO

Published by Pomegranate Artbooks,
P.O. Box 6099, Rohnert Park, CA 94927
Copyright ©1994 Sue Pierce and Verna Suit
All quilts copyright © individual artists.
All color photography by Breger & Associates.

WR BS DL JB

Library of Congress Cataloging-in-Publication Data
Pierce, Sue.
    Art quilts : playing with a full deck / Sue Pierce and Verna Suit.
        p.   cm.
    Quilts created for the Full Deck project and exhibition.
    Includes bibliographical references.
    ISBN 0-87654-300-X
    1. Full Deck (Project)—Catalogs.
    2. Quilts—United States—History—20th Century—Themes, motives—Catalogs.
    3. Playing cards in art—Catalogs. I. Suit, Verna. II. Full Deck (Project) III. Title.
    NK9112.P54   1995
    746.46'0973'07473—dc20   94-36681 CIP

Designed by Bonnie Smetts Design
Printed in Korea

contents

foreword

The Renwick Gallery of the Smithsonian Institution's National Museum of American Art is especially pleased to premiere the exhibition "Full Deck Art Quilts." Organized and circulated by the Smithsonian Institution Traveling Exhibition Service (SITES), the fifty-four quilted works will be on view from March 17 to April 30, 1995, prior to a national tour.

"Full Deck Art Quilts" simultaneously joins two historically rich traditions—decorating the surfaces of playing cards and quilt making—while it heralds the value of breaking away from those traditions. These innovative interpretations of cards in a non-playable fiber medium challenge our ideas about the imagery and functionality of both playing cards and quilts.

Today the quilt has become a form of contemporary expression that increasingly demands new and multileveled definitions. Diversity of ideas, materials, techniques and functions has forced the makers and their evaluators to discard simple definitions of function and warmth that the historical quilt comfortably provided. The power of the Full Deck project derives its strength through many facets that help define and clarify contemporary art quilting in the mid 1990s. Because of the diminutive size (28 x 18 in.) of these fifty-four interpretations, we immediately abandon the notion of functionality associated with full-scale quilts. By doing so, we are free to quickly move toward the power of the visual impact achieved by idea, color, material, composition, form and texture, much as we would when confronting a print, drawing or painting. By presenting these works in a radically altered size and by hanging them on walls as paintings, we acknowledge their power as image.

The unifying theme and the reduced scale of these quilted works has not compromised the integrity of vision and craft for which each artist is known. Because of their compactness, these works embrace an intensity of purpose and focus that might not have been achieved in the larger and more familiar quilt format. While most museums would not have the capacity to accommodate fifty-four full-sized quilts, they can exhibit these smaller pieces, thereby providing a rare opportunity to see the remarkable breadth of quilting as practiced in America today.

Contemporary quilt makers and those who appreciate their special talents owe a great debt to Sue Pierce for her conception of the Full Deck project. Like creating a quilt, having a vision is not enough unless it is combined with the technical skills necessary to bring that vision into reality. Sue Pierce's superb curatorial and organizational skills insured that this stunning collection is worthy of a museum exhibition, while her collaboration with Verna Suit on this handsome publication will endure long after the exhibition tour. Like each of the remarkable quilted pieces presented here, the Full Deck is vivid testimony that the whole is greater than the sum of the parts.

—Michael W. Monroe
Curator-in-Charge, Renwick Gallery

preface

Art quilting is a relatively new medium in the art world. When one thinks of a quilt it is usually as a bed-sized creation made using traditional designs and techniques. Artists are finding, however, that soft fabrics and the quilt format with its traditional associations can be very effective means of expression and that quilts can take on extraordinary power when seen in a different context. Art quilters are combining the principles of traditional quilting and their own sensibilities and training as artists to produce personal artistic statements.

Because of the comfort level and familiarity of quilts, however, the general public is not used to looking at them as art. Instead, art quilts often are admired for the number of hours required to construct them rather than for their design excellence or their thought-provoking content. One of the goals of the Full Deck is to increase the public awareness and appreciation of the art quilt medium by showcasing a broad range of art quilts in a collection that has inherent interest. More than being just another quilt show, the Full Deck is an accessible collection of artworks that has popular appeal.

Playing cards present an ideal theme for this purpose. They are part of our culture, and their images are universally recognized. They also come with a prepackaged set of symbols waiting to be interpreted: suits, num-bers, face cards and Jokers. The Full Deck affords a group of American artists working in the art quilt medium the chance to demonstrate their talents by playing with the familiar images of a deck of cards. Using the techniques of traditional quilting as a jumping-off place, they have transformed the fifty-two playing cards and two Jokers of a deck of cards into very contemporary, layered fabric artworks. This collection demonstrates that art quilters today are playing with a full deck of design talent, creativity and technical skill.

This collection offers an effective representative sampling of what is being done in the art quilt field today. The artists were chosen not as *the* definitive group of quilt makers but were selected for their individual strengths and for their general diversity of approach. They include many established and respected artists as well as some emerging talents. The fifty-four quilts speak not only for the participating artists but also for the many other talented people working in the art quilt medium.

Art Quilts: Playing With a Full Deck documents what might be considered a time capsule of art quilting at a certain time near the end of the twentieth century. A full-color reproduction of each of the fifty-four quilts is accompanied by an essay offering some background on the artistic philosophy and approach of the quilt's maker and a brief explanation of the techniques used to create each quilt. Additionally, the book draws on examples from the Full Deck to explore the imaginative use of the elements of a quilt and also of the various techniques employed by quilt artists today. In both the exhibitions and the book, the quilts are presented with the card order shuffled. The puzzle aspect of guessing their identities offers the viewer an incentive to look closely at the quilts and to think about them.

The Full Deck quilts are a great testament to creativity, a wonderful example of how fifty-four people can take an idea and carry it in as many different directions. The resulting variety of technical, interpretive and stylistic approaches guarantees that this collection will have something for everybody. Viewers are sure to find some quilts that communicate to them on a personal level, and isn't that really what art is about? The quilts will be seen first at the Smithsonian's Renwick Gallery and then will travel the country for three years. The hope of the Full Deck project is that these quilts will promote an appreciation both for the potential of quilting as a serious art medium and for the artists who created them and will provide inspiration for viewers' own creative natures. Undoubtedly, this collection will expand the perception of what a quilt is and what it can be.

acknowledgments

Foremost, I want to thank all of the very talented artists without whom there would have been no Full Deck. They had faith that the envisioned concept would become a reality. They made room for the Full Deck in busy schedules and devoted their creative energies to it, not as a quick diversion, but as a serious artistic challenge. They also endured with good grace the administrative trivia required to pull together a project of this scope. Their enthusiasm and ongoing support helped me get through the rough spots of pulling this whole project together. When what I had originally thought of as a six-month commitment began to gobble up several years of my life, it was the notes and calls from the artists that kept me going.

I am grateful to the Smithsonian Institution Traveling Exhibition Service (SITES) for seeing value in the Full Deck and selecting it from hundreds of other candidates as one of the exhibits they would package and make available to museums and galleries across the country. All of the SITES staff members have been a pleasure to work with and generous with their professional expertise. I am particularly indebted to project director Jacqueline Arendse, who patiently responded to all of my questions and suggestions.

Michael Monroe gave me some valuable advice early in the project and first put me in touch with SITES.

I also am most grateful for the thoughtful foreword he has written for this book.

Had not good fortune caused my path to cross with that of Verna Suit, this book might not exist, and surely not in its current form. She, too, had faith in the Full Deck project and maintained the necessary interest and energy to take on the challenge of documenting it. Through many hours of thoughtful discussion over our respective dining room tables or on the telephone, we gave coherence and structure to scattered and fragmented ideas. The final text is the product of the synergy created between my knowledge, experience and thoughts regarding the world of quilting and her analytical approach and talent with words.

As we prepared to venture into the world of publishing, Andrea Stevens of SITES provided invaluable advice, and Helene and Seymour Bress of Flower Valley Press gave us very welcome encouragement and tutelage. We were delighted that Pomegranate Artbooks chose to publish the book, and we thank Thomas Burke and the staff, and particularly editor Katie Burke, for making this a quality publication. Joel Breger and his associates provided excellent photography and good-humored support.

Many others made it possible for me to conceive and carry through with the Full Deck project, some by exam-

ple and others through active support. Charlotte Robinson demonstrated, by organizing "The Artist and the Quilt," that one person can take on a project of this scope and survive. Barbara Smith, who set the standard for excellence with her book *Celebrating the Stitch*, was generous with encouragement and advice. Dixie Rettig and Julianna Mahley freely shared some of the knowledge gained through hard work on a series of "Needle Expressions" exhibitions. Playing card collector Tom Dawson gave us the benefit of his expertise by reviewing the book's section on cards. My colleagues in New Image and also Fabric Vision have helped me to appreciate the "challenge" process and have given me invaluable personal and professional support. My children Laurie and Greg offered valued encouragement, and both family and friends cheerfully tolerated the fact that the Full Deck often took priority over my other obligations. Above all, Verna and I want to thank Brian Pierce and Dusty Suit, our live-in computer consultants and supportive spouses.

The Full Deck has been a cooperative project in many respects, and I hope that all of those who have contributed will share my pride and satisfaction in the results.

—Sue Pierce

how the full deck came about

As an artist, I have always enjoyed collective design challenges. They push me to try new things in my work, and the "high" I get from seeing other artists solving the same problems in different ways fuels my own creativity. In the fall of 1992 I was thinking about possible conceptual challenges with unifying themes and became intrigued with the idea of interpreting playing cards in fiber. Because of their familiar images and individual variety they seemed an ideal subject. Everyone has had some personal experience with playing cards. For instance, I have fond memories of games from my childhood and remember feeling proud when invited to play pinochle and canasta along with the adults. So I thought that cards might provide a rich source of personal associations and memories for other artists to mine while definitely posing a unique—but fun!—design challenge. Somehow, it seemed important that if any of the individual cards were to be created, the whole deck should be done. Although I initially had no thoughts of organizing a project with a national scope, I began to realize the potential of the idea and thus the Full Deck was born.

Those of us working in the emerging medium of art quilting, like artists in the past introducing new styles of painting, must help to create opportunities for our work to be seen and appreciated, even though most of us would prefer to spend all of our time and energy in the studio creating artwork. The creation of the Full Deck was entirely a grassroots effort. Excited about the project, I undertook its initial organization, with a goal of presenting a cross-section of some of the best work being done in the art quilt field. There was no outside funding; artists were asked to make a quilt for the collection and to pay for photography for documentation and promotion. I could promise them nothing in return except efforts to find appropriate venues in which to exhibit the finished collection.

After drafting project guidelines, I sent a letter of invitation first to selected artists whom I knew and whose work I respected, and then to artists whose work I had seen only in books and shows. To my delight, many of them accepted enthusiastically. "Deal me in!" replied one. In selecting artists, the goal was to achieve a good mix of different styles and, to some extent, a geographic distribution. Decisions became very difficult when it was time to issue the last invitations because clearly there were more talented artists than cards.

I was very pleased with the final list of people who committed themselves to making cards. They represented diverse backgrounds and styles. They were all serious artists who followed their own muse and would likely produce an intriguing collection of quilts. In no way did I set out to make this collection a feminist statement, but the truth is simply that the great majority of artists working in the quilt medium are women. In fact, the relative proportion of men and women in the Full Deck project may accurately reflect the population of art quilters. Coincidentally, the two men who are included among the Full Deck quilters happen to be halves of husband-and-wife teams, providing interesting examples of professional and domestic collaborations.

Artists were given the opportunity to select the card of their choice as long as it was available, and most of them replied with a prioritized list. Face cards often were the first choice because of their obvious symbolic potential. A few artists who prefer to do piecework asked for "something in Diamonds" because of the ease of working with the straight lines and geometric shape of that suit. Others chose number cards for their evenness or oddness, depending on whether they preferred symmetry or asymmetry in their compositions. Several artists asked for a Ten so they could have a maximum number of suitmarks to work with. To each new participant, I sent a welcome-to-the-project letter that included the actual card they had drawn. The card was partly a visual reminder and reference for the artist, but I also enjoyed the symbolic aspect of sending out a deck of card-stock playing cards and getting back a deck of quilts.

In creating project guidelines, I had tried to anticipate problems on the basis of my own experience as an exhibiting quilt artist and also my involvement in the administration of arts organizations. Decisions on details were often guided by practicality. For example, the modest size of the quilts (28 x 18 in.) would facilitate packing and installation and—with fifty-four pieces in the collection—would allow the quilts to be shown together at one time. The large size of many quilts that are created, often still referencing the size of a bed, limits the venues in which they can be displayed effectively. A small format would instead resemble that of paintings, and the show would fit comfortably into spaces designed for fine art.

Uniform size is, of course, a requirement for any deck of cards, but it would pose an additional planning challenge to quilt artists. Unlike a painter who starts with a canvas of given dimensions and fills it up, some art quilters start sewing fabric pieces together with only a general idea as to the size or shape of the finished piece. Even after construction of a quilt top is complete, additional shrinkage often occurs when the quilting stitches are added, and this would need to be factored into the planning. Later, it would become clear that the uniform size of the quilts also provided an effective format for comparison of individual artistic approaches.

In most cases I had no idea what particular artists had chosen to do with their cards and was therefore very curious to see the results. Few of the artists, either, knew what any of the others were doing. It was conceivable that several of them might coincidentally choose to interpret their cards in similar ways. How many of the quilts would follow the playing card format? How many would be based on traditional quilt design concepts such as repeated blocks?

It was very exciting when the completed quilts finally started arriving in the mail. As each was unwrapped from its packing, I truly marveled at how differently these artists, all working in the same medium, had interpreted their cards. This wonderful collection of quilts reinforces once again the infinite variety of possibilities in any situation and amply demonstrates that art quilters are "playing with a full deck," one packed with design talent, creativity and technical skill.

—Sue Pierce

the full deck in suit order

∫pade∫

Jane Burch Cochran

Deidre Scherer

Pat Autenrieth

Linda Levin

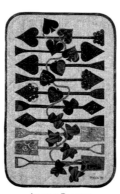

Jeanne Benson

Carolyn L. Mazloomi

Jean Ray Laury

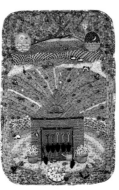

Natasha Kempers-Cullen

Gayle Fraas,
Duncan W. Slade

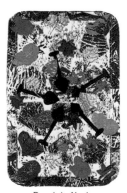

Dominie Nash

Sara Brown

Joan Schulze

Tafi Brown

12

Sandra Humberson

Diane Herbort

Elizabeth A. Busch

Holley Junker

Barbara Mortenson

Kathleen Sharp

Katherine McKearn

Linda S. Perry

Patty Hawkins

Yvonne Porcella

Lenore Davis

Robin Schwalb

Marguerite Malwitz

diamonds

Michele Vernon

Ardyth Davis

Lynne Sward

Karen Felicity Berkenfeld

Carol H. Gersen

Sue Pierce

Melissa Holzinger

B.J. Adams

Susan Ball Faeder

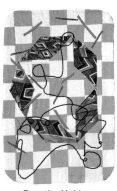

Dorothy Holden

Judy Becker

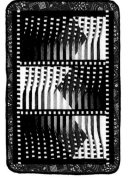

Caryl Bryer Fallert

Mickey Lawler

Libby Lehman

Joyce Marquess Carey

Therese May

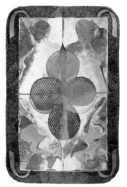

Emily Richardson

M. Joan Lintault

Deborah Melton Anderson

Katharine Brainard

Linda R. MacDonald

Jen Shurtliff

Chris Wolf Edmonds

Katherine Knauer

Dee Danley-Brown

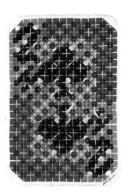

Jeanne Williamson

Kathleen O'Connor

Susan Shie, James Acord

CHAPTER 1

Art quilts

Art quilting is a modern art medium but one with ancient roots. The technique of quilting itself, joining fabric layers with stitching, has been used for centuries and in many variations throughout the world, but as both a hobby and an art form, quilting has especially flourished in the United States. In a country with democratic ideals quilting is truly a democratic craft, available to anyone with a pair of scissors, a needle and thread and some fabric. The choice of a quilt to memorialize AIDS victims indicates the strength of the national response to the quilting tradition.

The popularity of quilting in the United States may have something to do with the basic composite nature of both quilting and the country itself. A quilt's design traditionally is made by combining fabrics from many different sources, just as the melting-pot nature of the United States brings together many different cultural influences. In this way quilting is similar to jazz, another indigenous American art form. Both are improvisational and create new identities out of improbable parts, and both have evolved into a variety of complex styles.

The popularity of quilting today may also be in reaction to our increasingly technological modern life. The soft fabrics of quilts, with their sometimes nostalgic associations, contrast sharply with the ubiquitous plastic and metal of today's daily life, while the time-consuming stitching process of quilt making is in direct opposition to the expectation of instantaneous results of the electronic age. The original recycling theory of the quilting process itself, creating beauty out of scraps, also may be attractive to those rebelling against a throw-away society.

QUILTS AS ART

♣

In the last twenty-five or so years quilting has entered the realm of art. This is not to say that every quilt created is "art" but that quilting is a medium with the potential to be used as an art form. Artists are finding that fabric can take on extraordinary power when seen in a different context.

Art quilts are made using the principles of traditional quilting: building layers of fabric and connecting them with stitching. However, instead of being functional objects, art quilts have the postmodern quality of being self-referential; they celebrate the quality of "quiltness." They address both the long tradition of quilting, by retaining the quilt form's general parameters, and the present moment, by representing the artist's personal creative expression.

In art quilting, the medium is truly part of the message. Quilts traditionally have symbolized warmth and security and can therefore be an ironically effective format for calling attention to harsh realities. Art quilting, it has been said, provides a soft medium for tackling hard subjects. In a more straightforward way, medical centers and other organizations are trying to communicate their humanity by choosing quilts and other textiles as the artwork to decorate their walls. They are realizing that soft fabrics can warm cold, intimidating settings by providing a welcome contrast to glass and metal.

In many ways an art quilt can be seen as a soft alternative to a painting. An art quilt, like a painting, is generally made to be viewed hanging flat against a wall. Art quilts come in all sizes, as do paintings, and encompass a similar range of stylistic approach. They can be pictorial, narrative, abstract, impressionist, and so on. The standards by which one would judge a painting— such as composition, technical skill and authenticity of expression—are the same as would be used to judge an art quilt. Instead of a new painting style, art quilting is a new medium.

An interesting comparison can also be made between the art quilt and tapestry, another textile art form that has ancient roots but, unlike quilting, has long held a respected place in many museum collections. Both art quilts and tapestries are soft, flat, free-hanging fiber constructions, and they each have parallels with functional textiles. One could say that art quilts are to bed quilts what tapestries are to rugs. Similar weaving techniques have been used for centuries to create both functional rugs for the floor and decorative hangings for the wall. Likewise, the same quilting techniques are used to create warm quilts for the bed and art quilts for the wall. Contemporary artists who create either art quilts or tapestries are attracted by the soft, tactile quality of fiber and work within basic structural parameters; but like true artists in any medium, they seek to explore new territory and present original images and ideas. Art quilters are no more content to copy Baltimore Album quilts than are modern tapestry artists to reproduce images of unicorns.

An exhibition that played a landmark role in presenting quilts to the public as an art form instead of as a craft was the 1971 "Abstract Designs in American Quilts," which opened at the Whitney Museum of American Art in New York City. Although antique quilts were the focus of this show, they were hung on the walls in the manner of art paintings instead of displayed on beds or over the backs of chairs. Other quilt shows soon followed, often showcasing certain categories of quilts such as pieced, nineteenth-century or Amish. These shows inspired both artists and quilters either to explore the artistic possibilities of the quilting medium or to continue the creative work in fabric they had already tentatively begun.

The first show featuring contemporary quilts that had been produced by artists specifically as "art" may have been the 1975 exhibit "Bed and Board" at the DeCordova Museum in Lincoln, Massachusetts. The next year saw a similar show, "New American Quilts," at the Museum of Contemporary Crafts in New York City. Since then exhibitions of art quilts have been mounted with increasing frequency, both regionally and nationally.

A 1983 exhibit that traveled the country, "The Artist & the Quilt," paired well-known painters and other artists with quilt makers to produce collaborative art quilts. While this venture generated some controversy over the need to recruit "artists" to originate and guide the designs, the established reputations of these very artists opened the doors of museums and galleries that had never before shown quilts on their walls. It also prompted some writers and critics to actually look at art quilts for the first time.

A grassroots effort produced the first important juried competition specifically focusing on contemporary art quilts. The result was the 1979 Quilt National show, which inaugurated the Southeastern Ohio Cultural Arts Center, commonly known as The Dairy Barn. This competition has since become a biennial event with entries submitted from around the world. In addition to developing into the premier international showcase for contemporary quilts—with sections of it regularly touring the United

States and often abroad—it has become the standard by which other art quilt exhibitions are measured. Quilt San Diego is another important grassroots effort on behalf of art quilts. Its first juried competition was held in 1987, and it has since developed into a highly respected biennial event. Both Quilt National and Quilt San Diego have taken the important step of documenting their shows in published catalogs.

In the tradition of many new art movements that have appeared during the nineteenth and twentieth centuries, art quilters are recognizing the strength in unity. They have developed their own networks to support and encourage each other in their work and to further the public's appreciation of the art quilt medium. Nationally, quilt artists have formed such groups as the Studio Art Quilt Associates and several regional Art Quilt Networks that share information among members through newsletters and symposia. These groups work to gain recognition for art quilting and address such issues as the organization and promotion of serious exhibitions; methods of display, storage and shipping; and the encouragement of documentation and critical notice.

QUILT ARTISTS

♥

Art quilters have come to the medium through a variety of routes. Some artists who had been working in other media have switched to quilting because it offers them expressive possibilities they do not find in the more classic art forms. The soft, tactile, hands-on nature of quilting contrasts, for example, with the physically superficial process of applying pigment to the surface of a rigid, stretched canvas. Other quilt artists were first drawn to quilting to create functional bed covers and later turned the medium into a serious means of expression for their creativity.

The approach that art quilters take to their work is above all individual. Art quilters are subject to the same range of influences and inspirations as artists working in any medium. Stylistically, their work might reflect not only a particular art movement but also, by virtue of the fabric medium, traditional quilt patterning devices or the influence of other fiber arts. The subject matter of art quilts might be inspired by such varied things as personal relationships or experiences, social concerns, an impression of the moment or an image brought to mind by a piece of fabric. As in any medium, a complex blend of experiences, emotions, knowledge and sensibilities becomes the source of original creative work.

The actual working technique of quilt artists also varies widely. They may design their quilts carefully on graph paper or manipulate images on a computer. Or, they may compose a design more spontaneously and directly by experimenting with the placement of actual fabrics in a collage-type technique. Some artists choose to sew by hand, and others freely use the capabilities of the sewing machine. They sometimes incorporate unconventional materials and any of a variety of surface design techniques.

In the world of traditional quilting, emphasis is generally placed on excellence of technical skill—such as precision of seams and corners and fineness of stitching—and often the replication of traditional designs. While the perfection of quilting skills is important to the art quilter also, it is as a means to an end. Skills are mastered in order to be transcended. To an art quilter, the overall impact and statement of the quilt is of primary importance. The way a quilt is made gains significance from how it supports the quilt's message, not simply as a technical feat. Art quilters adapt traditional construction and design techniques to their own needs, using them as reference points rather than rules.

Quilt artists, like artists in any media, often work in series, shaping and reshaping images. They also feel free to change direction. Their work is constantly evolving, and many artists

in the field are now developing mature and very personal approaches to the medium. Techniques that they used in their early work may no longer be seen or may be used differently. Sometimes the techniques used by quilt artists overlap with other fields of art; a particular artist working in the medium of quilting could be just as easily termed an embroiderer, a painter or a maker of soft sculpture.

The fact that most art quilters are women is worth some speculation. It is not a surprising phenomenon considering that sewing and quilting have traditionally been women's tasks within the family. As a mother or wife, an artist has sometimes been in training for art quilting all her life, by sewing for her family and thus learning the basic skills. Impending motherhood has prompted many women artists to take up quilting in order to make baby quilts and then to continue to use the medium in their artwork. In other cases, pregnancy has influenced women artists to substitute quilting for painting because of concerns about possible health hazards connected with paints and solvents. In addition, the emphasis on feminism and women's studies during the last decades has helped to bring new appreciation for what has traditionally been looked on as a female craft.

Women have been both the originators and the leaders in the art quilt field, many of them teaching and sharing their techniques extensively. Special workshops taught by art quilters constitute virtually the only available instruction in the medium, since art quilting at this point is rarely taught in art schools. A number of art quilters have mentioned first working in the medium after being inspired and encouraged by other women quilt artists. Art quilting is an art form that is welcoming to women, particularly in comparison to fine art fields that are dominated by males, and often women choose it as their medium in response to something in their personal memory. As art quilter Sandra Humberson has said, "The needle is the instrument that connects generations of women, and our emotions to our lives, and has given us voice."

A feeling experienced by a number of art quilters early in their careers has been a personal need to validate themselves as artists. They frequently have been faced with the attitude that quilting is a craft suitable for a hobby or for home sewing or perhaps for a production business, but it is not "a real medium" for an artist to use. Art quilters are making the statement that it is. They have something to say, and fabric is their medium of choice. They believe in their work and let the work speak for itself.

pLAYINg witH a fuLL deck

PLAYING CARDS
♠

Creating new images for playing card designs has a long history. Since the forerunners of modern playing cards first made their European debut in the fourteenth century, cards have appeared in many regional variations. Face cards were drawn to resemble the nobility of nearly every country in which playing cards were manufactured until the designs became more or less standardized in the nineteenth century. The modern deck, known also as the "international" or "English" deck, is based on drawings of court figures from eighteenth-century France. Innovations such as double-headed images for two-directional readability, rounded corners for durability, corner indices for quick reference and the Joker as an added element of chance did not become common features until around 1880. The Joker actually was an American contribution, which has now spread to all standard "international" decks. While earlier decks normally had one Joker, modern decks typically contain two.

The symbols associated with the four suits also have been represented in a variety of ways. The suit known today as Spades, for example, has appeared at various times and in various countries as swords, pikes, leaves or shields. Hearts have been represented as cups or flowers. Clubs have appeared as wands, batons, rods, trefoils or acorns. And the suit of Diamonds, at one time or another, has been represented as rings, bells, coins, gold, money, squares and, in a Tarot deck, "pentacles."

Methods of playing card decoration through the years have paralleled contemporary developments in the graphic arts. The earliest cards were elaborately hand painted; later playing card production employed various methods of printing and stenciling that came into use. The name of the cards' maker was usually included in a scroll at the bottom, much as the Full Deck artists have each included their signatures on the cards in this quilted deck.

The artwork on cards frequently has been adapted to suit specific needs. After the French Revolution, Emperor Napoleon tried to replace the traditional royal designs with models of elegance and purity, and after the Russian Revolution the Soviets tried to replace them with revolutionary figures. Novelty cards have been designed for purposes of advertising, commemoration, education and even pornography.

A unique genre of playing cards known as "transformation cards" first appeared nearly two hundred years ago. In this tradition, the symbols and figures of the cards become integral parts of other designs. According to collector Albert Field, artists have been "transforming" playing card designs for artistic purposes since at least 1801.

The designs of nearly all early transformation decks were created around the suitmarks as they appeared on the cards, retaining the original placement and size of the suitmarks, or "pips," on number cards. In later years, innovative designers have treated suitmarks much more freely. Some recent transformation decks have been created by California artist Laura Sutherland in 1977, by fifty-four contemporary British painters in 1979, by American graphic artists in 1988 and by British artist Tony Meeuwissen in his "enchanted deck" of *The Key to the Kingdom* in 1992.

In short, playing cards are a natural subject for interpretation. The images are familiar to everyone, from children playing "go fish" to adults playing poker. Cards often evoke fond memories, such as intergenerational games of hearts or rummy at family gatherings or regular bridge games among friends. Sometimes the memories are bittersweet, such as the companionship of cards in a lonely game of solitaire.

Although there may be fewer afternoon bridge games today since more women are working outside the home, and children are more likely to be playing computer games than card games, playing cards remain a part of our culture. The expressions of card playing are part of our everyday language: "the deck is stacked," "play close to the vest," "show one's hand." The term "discard" was first used at the card table but is now a common verb. Playing cards are a mechanism for drawing people together. They are democratic, without class limitations or national boundaries, and the games that are played with them meet a variety of needs: an excuse for socializing, a vehicle for gambling, or intellectual stimulation.

The mystical, fortune-telling potential of playing cards is enhanced by the basic numerical structure of the deck, which begs to be given significance. For example, the fifty-two cards parallel the fifty-two weeks in a year; the four suits can be viewed as the four seasons, the four points of a compass or the four classic elements of earth, air, fire and water; and the total number of cards in a suit is the unlucky number thirteen. In addition, the face cards can suggest authority figures, parents, rivals, sons or lovers.

Playing card themes appear in all media. They have provided the titles and metaphors for movies, novels, popular songs and even classical music. In the visual arts, cards have appeared in paintings and tapestries and as motifs in wallpaper and upholstery. They have even been depicted in such a contemporary medium as polymer clay. However, this is surely the first time that an entire deck of cards has been quilted.

THE FULL DECK

◆

The Full Deck quilts were created individually by fifty-four American artists (actually fifty-six, since two quilts were collaborations) as an exhibit that would tour the United States. All were made in 1993, and, by a happy coincidence, this was the year that had been designated the Year of American Craft, in celebration of the creative work of the hand. Of course this is ironic, too, because art quilts constantly face the "art versus craft" debate in their struggle to be recognized as the artworks that they are. However, few people looking at the quilts in this collection would be tempted to term them "crafts." At a time when some of the leading artists in the field approach maturity in their art, gained by twenty or more years of experience, art quilts have come of age.

The Full Deck artists were chosen for their originality of design, mastery of technique and strong commitment to their work. They were selected with an eye to presenting a diversity of style in both interpretive and technical approach, and the list of participants includes artists from many parts of the country. All are professional quilt artists who show their work around the United States and sometimes abroad. Many lecture and teach workshops on quilt-related subjects. Some have written articles and books about quilting, and all have had their

work featured in various publications. Most work at their art full-time; only a few have careers not directly related to their artwork. The majority have had formal training in the fine arts. Among the participants there are some well-known names and also some emerging talents.

In approaching the design of the cards, artists were encouraged to make a quilt in a style that would be representative of their work. The piece could include any type of imagery as long as the information identifying the particular card was worked in as an integral part of the design. The main emphasis was that each quilt should be able to stand alone as a well-designed artistic expression.

The only restrictions imposed on the artists were that all quilts be uniform in size and shape and meet the definition of a quilt. The finished size of each quilt was to be 28 x 18 inches, proportional to a standard bridge card at a 14:9 ratio, and each quilt was to have rounded corners to mimic the shape of an actual card. For the purposes of the Full Deck project, the definition of an art quilt was stated as "a stitched construction of three or more layers using fabric as the primary material;" in other words, a "textile sandwich."

The fifty-four finished quilts represent a full deck of styles, techniques and materials. All of the pieces meet the broad definition of a quilt, although each is unique in the way it accomplishes its quiltness. Some pieces probably would not be called quilts by traditionalists. Several artists have freely used unexpected construction materials, such as Mylar, velveteen or heavy canvas, and others have enthusiastically embellished their pieces with not only beads and buttons but also leather, wood or metal. Some quilts were designed with holes in them, and the methods used for the quilting stitching that holds the layers together might best be described as idiosyncratic. But these are all free-hanging, three-layered textile sandwiches, and true to the nature of this soft, flexible medium, these quilted cards do not have the straight, rigid edges of their plastic-coated cardstock models.

This deck can be considered to be in the genre of transformation cards because the artists all have transformed the original playing card images to suit their own individual artistic purposes. Very often they have abstracted the card in some way: some omitted all or part of the corner index; others nominally referenced the card's identity but did not include the expected number of suitmarks or an actual face on a face card. While fully half of the artists retained the card's double-headed quality, many others opted for a single directional image for their quilts, often using the increased design freedom and extra space to create a narrative expression rather than a symbolic one.

A handful of quilts have all the expected elements of the real card: double-headed symmetry, the standard arrangement of suitmarks or figures and a corner index containing both letter or number and suit. However, in cases such as Joan Lintault's Ten of Clubs, one must look very closely before it is apparent that the quilt is a faithful representation of the card and that all the little clover Clubs are in their proper places. Jean Ray Laury's Eight of Spades may bear the most resemblance to a real card because of its traditional coloring and format, but, ironically, it is a visual joke that combines the features of both face card and number card, with Laury's own personal symbolism in the details. (Her tongue-in-cheek title for the card is "The Jean of Spades.")

Artists took a wide range of approach in the interpretation of their cards. In the case of the two Jokers, both artists drew on the card's function and symbolism. The Joker plays jokes; it can stand in for any card and thus influences the outcome of a game. Both quilted Jokers in this collection reference a character who can assume different identities and also have a capricious impact on destiny. Several artists worked with a card's aesthetic qualities within their own individual artistic styles or mined their personal emotional responses to cards' symbols. In this way, two sets of well-matched royal couples coincidentally appeared: both the King and Queen of Diamonds are represented by their initials, K and Q, and both the King and Queen of Spades are portraits of an artist's parent.

A number of artists enjoyed playing with visual puns by interpreting the cards' symbols literally. A Spade more than once became a tool for gardening, and a Heart, a vital organ. To Katherine Knauer a Club is a caveman's weapon; to Dee Danley-Brown it is something that men join. Susan Faeder's Diamond is a precious stone, while Karen Berkenfeld's is a place to play baseball. Joyce Marquess Carey's King of Clubs became a Communist despot in her "Red King in a Black Suit."

The Full Deck project has dealt these artists the chance to demonstrate their wide range of individual talents in creating this quilted deck, and, as you can see, they have played their cards well.

the artist's approach to quilt making

THE CREATIVE PROCESS

♣

How and when does the creative process begin for a new piece of art? The virtuoso performance of a musician at Carnegie Hall doesn't begin with the first note played but with the many hours of previous practice, and much the same can be said of the visual arts. Not only do artists need to acquire the skills to master the technical aspects of their work, but with "practice" they also build personal vocabularies of imagery and develop unique voices that are expressed through the objects they create. A body of work is often a continuum made up of discrete but connected pieces. The idea expressed in a quilt constructed in December may actually have been born while the artist was working on a different piece back in March or even several years earlier. Certainly each of the Full Deck artists began thinking seriously about possibilities for their card when they first received the invitation to participate, but as experienced artists, most happily brought into the process thoughts that had already been incubating in their creative minds.

Frequently artists sketch out several ideas as a sort of visual brainstorming approach, not knowing which will emerge as the best until they look at them all. Some artists regularly maintain a sketchbook as a journal of their ideas, for something

A page from the shared sketchbook of Susan Shie and James Acord

thought of last year and rejected for one project might be just what is needed months later for a different quilt. A page from the shared sketchbook of Susan Shie and James Acord plans the imagery for their Joker and also cheerfully notes that this was

written "on the way to Mohican State Park, in the sunshine." Sketchbooks might include drawings and notes as well as photos and clippings that inspire the artists or relate to the themes they are exploring. An artist's preliminary drawings can (and frequently do) range from rough thumbnail sketches on torn envelopes or napkins to exact plans drawn to scale.

Several of the Full Deck artists planned their quilts by computer. Joyce Marquess Carey used one to trace the image of Lenin's head from her source weaving. She then drew each component of the final picture (words, portrait, jacket, clubs, St. Basil's) as a separate "layer" in the program, moving things around and scaling them until she was happy with the composition. Finally, she scaled the whole drawing up to 28 x 18 inches to use as a guide to complete her quilt. Caryl Bryer Fallert likewise made good use of her computer and color printer to generate several possible variations before beginning the actual quilt construction.

The correlation between drawings and the finished quilt varies greatly. Although some artists make an exact pattern to follow, many others use a sketch as a map to chart direction. Even the best idea is constantly evaluated and modified in a search for the most effective way to express a concept in a strong aesthetic statement.

Some quilters develop a concept through many stages of increasingly detailed sketches, while others eschew paper entirely and take a direct and intuitive approach by starting out with fabric and scissors. Pin-up boards are fixtures in many quilters' studios. These are much like bulletin boards,

sometimes occupying an entire wall, and allow the artist to arrange and rearrange pieces of fabric and then step back to see the effect from a distance.

While most artists have a distinctive approach to the development of a project, they often take their methods for granted. All the Full Deck artists were encouraged to save drawings and notes in an attempt to document the process, but many had little to submit. This may reflect the spontaneity of many artists but may also indicate the emphasis they place on the finished piece of art and their tendency to minimize the struggle inherent in the creative process.

ELEMENTS OF A QUILT
♦

Among the characteristics of a creative mind is the urge to question known approaches to things and to push the limits of possibility. Creators of art quilts work within the basic framework of the quilt format (fabric layers joined by stitching), but they creatively manipulate each of the elements for their own purposes. The various techniques of quilting become tools for the artist's personal expression.

The Full Deck quilts are representative of the wide range of styles and techniques being used by art quilters today. Some of the artists worked in a very focused way within narrow parameters, while others freely combined many techniques. Some preferred to

disregard or even defy the neatness and order that is emphasized in much traditional quilting by leaving raw fabric edges exposed and threads unclipped. The variety of ways in which the artists took advantage of quilting's potential to achieve different effects offers a glimpse of the infinite possibilities of this medium and of artistic creativity.

....

FABRIC
Freedom of choice for art quilters begins with basic construction materials. Early quilters worked with cotton fabric for both the design-carrying quilt top and the backing because it was affordable, accessible and durable. For today's art quilters, any textile becomes a potential quilting material. Many still prefer to use 100 percent cotton, however, for its natural integrity and feel in the hand, its reputed "ease of needling" and its ability to accept dye and fabric paint.

Not content to draw only from the colors and patterns available in commercially produced fabrics, many artists gain increased control over their basic materials by dyeing or painting fabrics to their own taste. Carol Gersen, for instance, dyes all of the fabrics that she uses in her work. For the Ten of Diamonds she created a range of autumn reds for her leaves and blues for her sky that rival Mother Nature's best. Caryl Bryer Fallert also frequently dyes her fabrics, as she did to produce the close shades of gray that progress across the pleats in the Three of Diamonds. For the Eight of Hearts, Katherine McKearn overdyed a number of commercial prints, retaining their original patterns but changing them into a cohesive family of reddish fabrics appropriate to a red suit. Emily Richardson painted a variety of fabrics in four basic colors that she then used to create a collage with a quadripartite quality.

Instead of altering the overall color of the cloth, other artists customize fabric by creating unique patterns using dyes or paints applied with brushes or other tools. Sara Brown customized her fabric for the Four of Spades using the batik wax-resist method of dyeing to add words and images that reinforce her message. Several times a year, Linda Levin uses a variety of painting techniques to customize many yards of fabric in advance, which she draws upon for later projects, such as her Jack of Spades. Mickey Lawler used a variety of unorthodox methods and tools to create color and textural effects for the ethereal background of her Two of Diamonds. In addition to using her hand-painted fabrics in her own work, Lawler has built a business out of selling her unique yardage to other quilt makers.

For some quilt artists, commercially printed fabric is the material of choice. They value fabric that comes to them already carrying information, and the search for the right materials becomes an important part of the artistic process. Like dyers or painters mixing colors to achieve a certain shade, they look for solid or patterned fabrics that provide the desired sense of color and texture and perhaps a subliminal message with cultural or emotional content. In the Three of Clubs, Dee Danley-Brown's use of cutouts from a commercially printed fabric for the little figures of plodding businessmen makes a satirical comment on their cookie cutter sameness. Lynne Sward brought together many tiny pieces of commercial fabric to create a confetti-like collage of cultural references for her Queen of Diamonds. Sue Pierce and Kathleen Sharp both employed commercial fabrics to suggest building materials. Through the artists' careful choices of pattern and color, soft fabrics with designs originally intended for use in clothing or upholstery instead suggest the hard surfaces of stone and wood.

In the work of several Full Deck artists, fabrics from other times or places contribute to the message through their history or the associations they evoke. Carolyn Mazloomi regularly chooses textiles that reflect her African-American heritage, a significant part of her personal artistic statement. Sara Brown used remnants of fabrics she collected while living abroad to create a Four of Spades that is a testament to parts of the world torn by violence. Patricia Autenrieth's poignant portrait of her mother includes scraps from one of her mother's dresses and fabrics reminiscent of those she might have worn. In the Ace of Spades, Jane Burch Cochran incorporated patchwork blocks from an antique quilt and actual gloves that call up images of southern womanhood and impart a sense of history. Such reuse of materials also recalls the recycling approach that often went into the creation of early patchwork quilts.

Artists sometimes choose nontraditional fabrics for the benefit of their physical qualities. Melissa Holzinger's Eight of Diamonds, made with artist's canvas and painted with acrylic paints, resembles a Log Cabin pieced quilt, but her bold, aggressive materials contradict the pattern's traditional homely image. At the other extreme, Barbara Mortenson and Emily Richardson took advantage of the semitransparent qualities of fabrics such as silk sheers and cotton gauzes, layering them to create effects of depth and half-hidden secrets. Holley Junker used shiny circles of brightly colored Mylar to suggest the lights and crowds of a city in which a fleeing Knave of Hearts hopes to lose himself.

....

BACKING

In addition to the "quilt top" that carries the design, a quilt has a second fabric layer on its underside, called the "backing." This layer often is not visible: in a traditional quilt it faces the bed; in an art quilt it usually faces the wall. It is primarily a finishing touch that completes the "textile sandwich," providing a smooth surface to the underside and hiding any "process" work. It also provides a foundation for the compression produced by the quilting stitches, thereby helping to create a quilt's insulating air pockets and the three-dimensional quality of its design.

To a quilt artist, the backing is still another facet of the total design, albeit a secondary one. When elaborate quilting has been done, a plain backing will set off the intricacy of the stitching pattern. However, many artists choose to relate the backing in some way to the quilt top, such as by piecing it out of the same fabrics or by including elements of the quilt top's imagery. Several Full Deck artists, for instance, have backed their quilts with commercial fabric printed with images of playing cards. Kathleen Sharp appliquéd a label to the back of her quilt on which she had embroidered names for her nine Hearts (Stout, Light, Dear . . .). Early quilters occasionally used the backing in this way to add an explanation of a quilt's origins or authorship. In many ways, the usually unseen backing can be made to offer a delightful surprise when it is revealed by chance.

BATTING

Between the two outer layers of a quilt is an invisible third layer of batting. In a traditional quilt intended for use on a bed, the batting layer adds loft for maximum insulation and warmth. When it is compressed by the quilting stitches, the padding of the batting layer plays an aesthetic role by helping to emphasize the patterns made by the stitching. Batting is commonly made of cotton or polyester, although wool or silk batting can be found occasionally, and it comes in various thicknesses.

For an art quilter, even the batting layer becomes a design element to be manipulated. Jean Ray Laury used a layer of yellow felt, both to serve as batting and also to create a narrow inner border around the edge of her Eight of Spades. Since the batting layer is not usually intended to be seen, some artists all but ignore it and include only a token batt, perhaps a piece of cotton flannel or some other cloth. If an artist has used a muslin base to support the quilt top, such as in a collage-type design, sometimes the muslin takes the place of the middle batting layer. On the other hand, Sandra Humberson, Dee Danley-Brown and Deborah Anderson all included extra batting to give a three-dimensional quality to parts of their designs.

QUILTING

Another necessary element of a quilt is the stitching that gives the genre its name. The technique of stitching layers together, or "quilting," gives stability to the multilayered construction by anchoring the components at intervals. In addition, the stitching plays an important aesthetic role. Stitches can give emphasis to pieced or appliquéd fabric shapes by following their outlines, can superimpose separate patterns as additional design elements or can create a unifying textural quality over the whole quilt or a limited area. Quilting is the frosting on the cake. When a quilt top undergoes the final quilting process, a once flat fabric design takes on life as it gains subtle dimension.

Artists explore the design possibilities of the quilting element in endless ways, beginning with their choice of methods and materials. For the stitching itself they may choose to work either by hand or machine. A sewing machine's speed, versatility and strong, even stitches often make it a valuable tool, but sometimes hand quilting is the technique of preference to gain a desired aesthetic effect. Quilting by hand also can provide an artist with a tactile personal link to the quilt.

The actual thread that artists use for quilting often remains an unobtrusive cotton or polyester-wrapped sewing thread, valued for its function in creating designs rather than any intrinsic decorative property. However, artists sometimes choose to accentuate their stitches. They may add color by stitching in various hues, enliven a quilt with the sparkle of metallic thread or add texture by stitching with some heavier material. In Susan Shie and James Acord's Joker, bundles of embroidery floss create bold, riotous quilting stitches that contribute to the total tactile quality of their quilt.

The pattern created by the quilting stitches is another significant design element. The technique of outlining pattern elements with quilting stitches is a popular and effective way of accentuating a shape. This technique was used to great advantage, for example, by Jen Shurtliff, who quilted around each mosaic tile in her Six of Clubs, giving such dimensional relief that it is hard to believe the tiles are merely painted shapes. Jean Ray Laury used this outlining technique in the Eight of Spades to a different effect. With tiny hand stitches reminiscent of traditional quilting, she neatly traced the classic shapes of her playing card, emphasizing the apparent conventionality of her unconventional card and quilt.

Some artists produce quilting that is virtually invisible. Michele Vernon chose the uncluttered "in the ditch" technique of stitching over seams to underscore the pristine sharpness of her Ace of Diamonds. Ardyth Davis quilted her King of Diamonds in

flowing lines of metallic thread that meld with the contours of her rich, manipulated fabric. Other artists, such as Dominie Nash and Barbara Mortenson, have added no separate quilting at all, choosing instead to let appliqué or embroidery stitches do double duty as quilting.

Quilting can be an integral part of the quilt top design or can reinforce imagery. Susan Faeder's quilting lines trace the sparkle from the facets of her cut Diamond stones, and Mickey Lawler's mark the circular orbits of her red Diamond stars. Kathleen Sharp's blocklike quilting on the walls in her Nine of Hearts divides solid pieces of fabric into building stones. Carolyn Mazloomi stitched the shapes of African masks into the background of her quilt, continuing the theme set by her African fabrics and incidentally making her Nine of Spades a subtle double-headed face card.

A traditional role of quilting stitches is to add an overall unifying pattern to the various fabrics of a quilt top. Linda Perry took this approach in stitching over the whole surface of her Seven of Hearts in a unique angular pattern that is in keeping with the art deco feeling of her composition. Lenore Davis adapted a tailor's collar stitch as a unifying element for the printed motifs on her Four of Hearts, using a stitch in scale with a subtle grid pattern that underlies parts of her quilt's surface.

In other instances, artists have used quilting stitches as patterning to differentiate, emphasize or add texture to parts of their designs. Gayle Fraas and Duncan Slade illuminated their scenes of unspoiled wilderness with rows of gold metallic quilting. Kathleen O'Connor used quilting to further individualize fabrics in her disharmonious Joker. Sue Pierce quilted a wall area in a meandering free-form design to suggest the texture of crumbling plaster, while Libby Lehman used a similar technique with gold thread to create a rich, gold-encrusted background for her jewellike Ace of Clubs.

In the Full Deck project, quilting patterns were used several times to reinforce card identities. In Yvonne Porcella's Five of Hearts, quilting stitches form a subtle figure 5 as a corner index. Carol Gersen quilted background Xs as Roman numeral tens to identify her card's number and to harmonize with the Diamond shape of its suitmark. Judy Becker quilted Diamond shapes as an added refrain in background areas of her Four of Diamond blocks, and Marguerite Malwitz quilted flying bird motifs to echo the elusive heart shapes in her Two of Hearts.

QUILT TOP CONSTRUCTION TECHNIQUES

♠

Traditionally, there have been two basic methods for creating a quilt top: piecing and appliqué. Contemporary quilt makers have expanded the design possibilities by exploring approaches such as decorating whole cloth and manipulating fabrics. Various quilt artists in the Full Deck project have made use of each of these. However, with the creative freedom that is an artist's province, they regularly adapted methods for their own purposes, combined several techniques in one quilt or invented new methods of their own.

PIECING

Probably the most common perception of a quilt is the traditional American patchwork or "pieced" quilt, in which the quilt top is constructed of small pieces of fabric, usually cut in regular geometric shapes, that are stitched together to form a pattern. These individual fabric pieces combine to form an actual fabric layer of the quilt and are seamed together to create a neat, flat surface.

In the Full Deck project, several artists used pieced construction exclusively. Michele Vernon used this traditional technique in a very straightforward form, constructing her Ace of Diamonds entirely of rectangular

blocks all the same size. However, she formed some of her blocks by joining two triangles, and her resulting diagonal lines and careful color choices combine to suggest the Diamond shape, its interior facets and even corner indices. Judy Becker used a similar block construction technique, but with squares and rectangles of varying sizes and several simple, repetitive patterns within the blocks. Carol Gersen's more free-form piecing resulted in a subtle composition that reflects meticulous control. It is not coincidental that all three of these pieced quilts interpret cards in the suit of Diamonds, since that suitmark's straight lines lend themselves to joining along seamlines more readily than do the curves of Hearts, Clubs or Spades.

Sections of patchwork are sometimes included in quilts because of the traditional nature of the technique and the nostalgic connections it can evoke. In Jane Burch Cochran's country garden scene, a patchwork field of antique fabrics awaits digging by her button-trimmed garden Spade. Therese May pieced a border suggesting a braided hearth rug to surround images stemming from her childhood dreams. Dorothy Holden's simple pieced background with inexactly aligned squares emphasizes her quilt's feeling of ingenuousness. And Dee Danley-Brown pieced an immediate foreground of simple, harmonious squares that suggest a less frantic and stressful world outside the stark grids of the city.

Piecing can serve an artist's needs by providing a means for mixing colors and patterns to provide a cumulative effect that has depth and interest. Libby Lehman's patchwork background in jewel tones adds to the overall richness of her Ace of Clubs. Patty Hawkins adapted the strip-piecing technique—in which various fabric strips are sewn together and the resulting striped fabric cut crosswise to produce a strip made up of different patches—to create a generally yellow background for her Six of Hearts. To this she added appliqués of strip-pieced Hearts that are generally pink and generally red, producing a composition with an overall feeling of warmth and sunshine. Linda Levin used a similar strip-piecing technique in parts of her Jack of Spades. The resulting intricacy of Jack's curls provides a textural contrast to the quilt's random, spattered background, and further strip-piecing suggests a detailed cuff to his sleeve. Chris Wolf Edmonds pieced a

Carol Gersen's drawing board with full-size template underneath the almost complete pieced quilt top for the Ten of Diamonds. Photo by Carol Gersen.

background for her Five of Clubs with strips of color and pattern that evoke a winter landscape with a regularity that suggests a furrowed field.

Piecing can also provide sharp definition. Susan Faeder carefully pieced her appliquéd Diamonds to show the facets of the cut stones, employing fabrics that further suggest inner sparkle and life. Yvonne Porcella pieced together the gaming table that forms a background for assorted appliqués in her Five of Hearts and used strip piecing in its classic application to create the checkerboard.

....

APPLIQUÉ

The term appliqué, the French word meaning "applied," indicates something that is added. In quilting the term is used to describe fabric ornamentation that is sewn to the surface. Since this design technique does not have the restriction of individual elements needing to physically fit together as in piecing, appliqué allows an artist increased freedom of composition. Instead of the straight edges typical of piecing, fabric shapes for appliqué are more likely to be cut with curved and irregular edges, as in the appliquéd flowers and wreaths of traditional Baltimore Album quilts. In the Full Deck project, Jeanne Benson's Ten of Spades comes closest in feeling to the traditional style of flat, familiar shapes against a solid background. However,

she has modernized her design by transforming the images Escher-fashion and attaching and overcasting the edges of the appliqués with a machine-sewn satin stitch instead of sewing by hand with traditional turned-under hems.

Machine appliqué is a popular technique among art quilters, both for its speed and for the effects that can be achieved with machine-stitched thread. Katharine Brainard, Kathleen O'Connor, and Sue Pierce all used a thick satin stitch in various colors to attach appliquéd shapes as well as to outline them and thus impart a cartoonlike character to the resulting pictures. Deidre Scherer outlined elements of her King of Spades with satin stitching and used a zigzag stitch in varying

lengths and colors to blend the appliqué pieces that form the contours of her King's face. In the Queen of Hearts, Elizabeth Busch appliquéd canvas cutouts with a large, rough zigzag stitch. Her crude construction elements combine to suggest childish valentines cut from construction paper.

Other artists revel in the detail and intricacy possible with hand-appliqué. Jane Burch Cochran, for example, accented her functional appliqué stitches with bugle beads. Robin Schwalb stitched appliqué elements to her Three of Hearts with such a fine hand that it is difficult to tell them from the stenciled portions of her carefully drafted design.

This photo of the Queen of Clubs shows fabric shapes pinned to the background cloth in preparation for being sewn in place. Also pinned in place is a drawing of the central figure, which will be used as a pattern for additional fabric appliqués.

The ancient technique of reverse appliqué, cutting away fabric to reveal other layers beneath, has been used for centuries by the Hmong people of Laos in their traditional needlework, and the San Blas Indians of El Salvador for their colorful molas. It also was employed by Full Deck artists Deborah Anderson and Libby Lehman. Lehman used the technique to disclose the depths of fire within her jewellike Club, while Anderson cut away fabric and batting from the negative spaces surrounding her Clubs to give them dimension and reveal a highly textured background.

Many artists who choose to work in appliqué use a composition technique similar to collage in that they completely cover a blank muslin base with overlapping fabric shapes. Often raw fabric edges will be left exposed, adding to a general feeling of spontaneity. Marguerite Malwitz used this approach in creating a tranquil Bermuda beach scene with fabrics and motifs suggestive of an island paradise, while Kathleen O'Connor stressed her Joker's disharmonious nature through a collage of contrasting fabrics and aggressive shapes. Emily Richardson additionally took advantage of the overlapping aspect of collage by layering semitransparent fabrics to suggest a Jack of Clubs with subtle complexity. Deidre Scherer used a similar layering approach to sculpt the planes of her King's face. Kathleen Sharp's layered

Emily Richardson worked on a pin-up wall to position layers of translucent fabrics as the Jack of Clubs was constructed.

shapes combine with the perspective of her tile floor to create the illusion of a hallway's depth.

A somewhat different approach to the collage appliqué method was taken by Diane Herbort, Holley Junker and Lynne Sward. Instead of attaching the fabric shapes by stitching around the edges of each, these artists positioned many small appliqués to overlap each other and cover the muslin background and then attached them all at one time using some method of overall stitching. Each artist's procedure was unique. The effect of each, however, mimics both the cumulative brush strokes of a painting and the piecing technique of joining many small pieces of fabric.

Other artists used appliqué methods that closely resemble traditional piecing techniques. Melissa Holzinger's seemingly traditional Log Cabin pattern for the Eight of Diamonds was actually created through appliqué, as was the strip-pieced effect in the chevron-patterned background of Sandra Humberson's complex Ace of Hearts.

WHOLE CLOTH QUILTS
The whole cloth quilt might be considered a philosophical departure from the usual concept of a quilt because it does not combine different fabrics. The quilt top is a solid piece of fabric that carries the design itself instead of

This detail of Caryl Bryer Fallert's "Checking Over the Rainbow III" shows her use of twisted pleats to add dimension and interest to the quilt's surface.

deriving it from appliquéd shapes or the seaming together of fabric pieces. It is "cut from whole cloth" in the truest sense of the phrase. An artist who creates a whole cloth quilt takes a design approach similar to that of a painter starting with a blank canvas. Traditionally, whole cloth quilts have acquired their decoration from patterning made by quilting stitches or by embroidery. With the great variety of surface design methods and materials available today, and the willingness of artists to freely employ them, whole cloth art quilts can take many forms.

Frequently a whole cloth quilt fools the viewer's eye through some trompe l'oeil aspect that suggests another means of quilt construction or design. Jen Shurtliff created the mosaic tiles of her Six of Clubs entirely with paint,

enhancing the visual deception through the dimensional relief of the quilting. Gayle Fraas and Duncan Slade's complex Six of Spades appears to have a border of printed cloth, but in actuality this is painted onto their whole cloth quilt with the same dyes they used to paint the wilderness landscapes. They added a further illusion by painting shadows behind elements of their design. Natasha Kempers-Cullen painted sections of her pastoral scene in such a discrete way that they appear to be cut from different pieces of fabric. Similarly, collaborators Susan Shie and James Acord created very convincing illusions of texture in their painted whole cloth Joker, causing individual design elements to appear to be appliquéd fabric shapes. Other leather and clay embellishments that actually are sewn to the surface compound the viewer's uncertainty.

Several Full Deck artists created whole cloth quilts that reference traditional piecing and appliqué techniques through their use of symmetry and repeated shapes and motifs. Lenore Davis used various printing, painting, rubbing and stenciling techniques to produce a center medallion that mimics piecework and four corner Hearts that look like appliqués. Katherine Knauer's stenciled cavemen motifs recall symmetrical appliqué patterns usually associated with more conventional subject matter. Jeanne Williamson's stamped Two of Clubs could be a pieced quilt conceived by a computer.

MANIPULATED FABRICS

Although quilts lie flat against a bed or a wall, they are not exactly two-dimensional. They gain a third dimension through the building up of fabric layers and batting, and this quality of depth is emphasized by the compression of the quilting stitches. The layers of appliqué, the loose threads of fabric edges left raw and the implied turned-under seam allowances of piecing also can add subtle depth. Some quilters add more overt dimension to their quilts by folding, pleating or physically manipulating the fabric in some other way, creating a variety of textural effects and patterns. The traditional Cathedral Window pattern is termed "manipulated" because its pattern is a result of methodical folding.

Among the Full Deck artists, Caryl Bryer Fallert manipulated her fabrics for the Three of Diamonds by sewing a succession of two-sided pleats on the quilt's surface and reversing their directions mid-pleat, creating a feeling of oscillating movement and depth. In the King of Diamonds, Ardyth Davis used a smocking machine to press fine pleats into silk fabrics, which retain the memory of their pleating in the form of an undulating ripple texture that is rich with the nuance of reflected light. Deborah Anderson added textural depth and complexity to the background of her Nine of Clubs through subtle, irregular tucks that remain in place.

Linda MacDonald applies acrylic paints with an airbrush, using stencils and grids to create some of her unique surface patterning.

Katherine McKearn manipulated an additional aspect of dimensionality by giving her Eight of Hearts a discontinuous surface. Besides tightly gathering her fabrics, which communicates both the tension of compressed energy and the spontaneity of folk art, she cut away the negative spaces around her designs through all the quilt's layers, leaving empty space through which the wall behind can be seen. She also cut out the eye holes of her Heart-shaped masks, making them actual functioning false faces. Joan Lintault's Ten of Clubs is another example of a quilt that does not have a continuous surface. In her case, she created small, stuffed, individual elements and later assembled them, a constructional approach not unlike that used in traditional Yo-Yo quilts.

SURFACE DECORATION TECHNIQUES

♥

Quilt artists are finding an infinite variety of inventive ways to decorate or create designs on the surface of fabrics. They employ many variations of the surface design techniques of painting and printing, using textile paints, inks, dyes and even standard acrylic paints as colorants. The Full Deck artists applied color and pattern with brushes, squeeze bottles and other assorted tools and a wide variety of printing methods. They drew on surfaces with oil pastels, fabric markers and even colored pencils. Many artists also took full advantage of the design possibilities of stitchery and embellishment. They attached beads,

buttons and more unconventional materials, both to add surface interest and as major elements of their designs. To an art quilter, practically any design technique or material is potentially useful if it creates a desired effect.

PAINTING

Many Full Deck artists used painting techniques at various stages of their designs, from the fabric painters who cut their painted cloth into pieces to the whole cloth painters who left their creations intact. Elizabeth Busch, Chris Wolf Edmonds and Michele Vernon incorporated painting techniques in their quilts by juxtaposing pieces of their hand-painted fabrics with commercial fabrics. Mickey Lawler, Linda Levin and Joan Schulze pieced or appliquéd backgrounds of hand-painted fabrics that they further ornamented by assorted surface design methods. Therese May painted much of her quilt's background in a whole cloth approach, added appliqués and then painted other designs on top of everything.

Various painting techniques proved valuable to Full Deck participants both for creating design elements and adding finishing details. Karen Berkenfeld, Lenore Davis and Linda MacDonald used fine brushwork to accentuate and sharpen details of designs produced by printing and stenciling. Yvonne Porcella used a brush to paint the details of her bottle of Hearts #5

 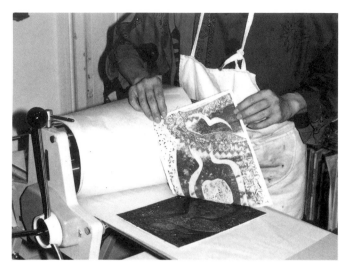

After designing her plates, Karen Berkenfeld uses an etching press to print on cotton fabric.

beer, as did Chris Wolf Edmonds to add fringe to her spiral designs and to dab an ethereal background 5. Katherine Knauer, Linda MacDonald and Jen Shurtliff all made extensive use of airbrushing in combination with stencils or resists to create their patterns. Robin Schwalb's classic composition is composed of stenciled design elements that she added through appliqué and also details that she stenciled directly to the quilt's surface. Sue Pierce diluted acrylic paint and applied it like a stain to further age the ancient wall in her street scene. Ardyth Davis applied a color wash shibori-fashion over compressed silk pleats to suggest brushed gold. Jane Burch Cochran took a very direct approach to applying color in her down-to-earth Ace of Spades by dipping part of a glove into green textile ink to produce a green thumb.

PRINTING AND PHOTO TRANSFER

An increasing number of artists are incorporating various methods of printing in their quilts, reproducing patterns and images from other sources to use as surface design on their fabric. Some use printing techniques to add small details, while for others printing is the primary design method. Some artists use ancient techniques and others experiment with modern technology. In the Full Deck project, printed effects range from the textural areas created by Barbara Mortenson and Lenore Davis through rubbing to the integrated original artwork and photographs of Jean Ray Laury.

One of the advantages offered by printing is the capability of applying whole images in a unit process. Full Deck artists have used this capability in a variety of creative ways. Diane

Herbort used commercial rubber stamps to print fabric with familiar images relating to her Heart suit (hearts, red lips), later randomly cutting the fabric into small pieces to be appliquéd in her scrap-bag collage technique. Marguerite Malwitz used commercial stamps to carefully place a line of palm trees on a hill and a shell on the sand in her idyllic beach scene. For the Queen of Diamonds, Lynne Sward photocopied many images relating to both queens and diamonds and used them as scattered motifs in her whimsical collage. Lenore Davis used a mono-printing technique to create an arrangement of discrete patterns in the central medallion of her Four of Hearts, as if she were piecing together this part of her whole cloth quilt from individual quilt blocks.

Several other artists manipulated

photographic transfer processes to print fabrics with images whose associations added subtle meaning to their quilts. Joan Schulze silkscreened greatly enlarged photographs of the city where her mother lived to give a worn, faded quality to the pips on her Three of Spades, in tribute to her mother's old cards. Dominie Nash customized all the fabrics that she used by silkscreening enlarged photo-

The absolute realism offered by photographic transfer methods was used to reference specific personalities in several Full Deck quilts. Elizabeth Busch reproduced photographs of her children and of herself as a child to take pride of place in the center of her Queen of Hearts. Jean Ray Laury created her own private face card by crowning photographic transfers of herself in a double-headed central

a principle central to the designs of many traditional quilts. Printing also offers a precision that can approximate the effect produced by a machine. In the Jack of Diamonds, Karen Berkenfeld used a block-printing technique with carved linoleum blocks to create repeated images of action figures that suggest the frames of a film strip, and to stamp Brooklyn Dodger logos that re-create the printed cloth of a faded baseball uniform. Gayle Fraas and Duncan Slade produced the suggestion of commercially printed fabric in the border of the Six of Spades by stamping uniform spade motifs with a hand-carved rubber eraser. Jeanne Williamson also used carved erasers as a stamping tool to mimic computer-screen pixels in creating her entire Two of Clubs.

Jeanne Williamson cuts rubber erasers into shapes, applies fabric paint to the eraser with a brush and then hand stamps each area of color onto the cloth. After one layer of paint has dried, she often prints a second layer of overlapping printed shapes to create the complex overall design of her whole cloth quilts.

graphic images of flowers and garden scenes and producing a complex Five of Spades with an organic, earthy feeling. Tafi Brown personalized her Two of Spades with a background of white pine branches from her own yard, printing the fabric using her trademark Cyanotype technique.

medallion on her Eight of Spades. Lenin becomes the archetypical King of Clubs through photo-transfer in Joyce Marquess Carey's "Red King in a Black Suit."

Another advantage offered by printing is the capability of repeating a motif the same way multiple times,

Other artists printed multiple images that reflect the eternal repetitions of the natural world. Joan Lintault used a silkscreen technique to produce many identical clovers and other tiny plants and critters for her Ten of Clubs, as did Sandra Humberson to endlessly echo the word "memory" in her Ace of Hearts. Natasha Kempers-Cullen stamped many little spade-shaped leaves for her trees. Barbara Mortenson photocopied a picture from a book to create ten anatomically correct Hearts. Chris Wolf Edmonds carved wooden blocks to print five spirals symbolizing the inevitable progress of life from birth to death.

Sandra Humberson hand screenprinted many fabrics using screens with the word "memory" repeated to form a pattern. She printed fabrics in various combinations of the "card" colors of black, red and white. They are seen here both pinned to the print table and hanging on the wall. Those not needed for her Ace of Hearts will be used in other projects.

EMBROIDERY

Embroidery is a natural technique for decorating the surface of a quilt. The basic needle-and-thread sewing process is essentially the same for both construction and embroidery, but embroidery is unique in that its value lies in the decorative effect of the thread itself rather than in any functional role of the stitches. In the past, some traditional quilts have been decorated exclusively with cross-stitch.

Art quilters are finding many ways of integrating this closely related technique into their fabric designs. Some

use it to add small details, such as the running stitches representing hand-quilting in Melissa Holzinger's quasi-traditional Log Cabin pattern, or the metallic chainstitching with which Ardyth Davis gilded some of the silk ripples in her King of Diamonds. In other cases it is difficult for the viewer to tell whether the stitches on a quilt's surface are functional or whether they are placed on the surface purely as decorative or design elements. Frequently stitches serve more than one purpose. Sue Pierce, for example, used a machine-sewn satin stitch to appliqué design elements in her Nine of Diamonds as well as to embroider

an outline around the fabric shapes in a contrasting color for emphasis. She also used embroidery in its classic role as a drawing line to add details to her picture, and in some cases it assumes a dual role as part of the quilting.

The capabilities of modern sewing machines are influencing some quilt artists to use embroidery as a major design technique in their work. B. J. Adams used an industrial sewing machine to cover most of a pieced canvas surface with closely spaced rows of satin stitching to create a complex and vibrant Seven of Diamonds. Patricia Autenrieth used her sewing machine much as a pencil or crayon to draw the central figure and many other design elements of her Queen of Spades. Libby Lehman employed freehand machine embroidery techniques to add the illusion of fire within her jewellike Ace of Clubs, as well as to give a filigree effect to the card's background and to add lacy corner indices. With surgical precision, Barbara Mortenson's machine-embroidered lines sculpt realistic Hearts and trace veins and arteries as they disappear into fabric tissues.

Embroidery has long been a useful technique for adding text to a fabric surface. Many quilt makers of the past have documented their work with embroidery, and in the Full Deck project it was frequently the method of choice for signing a work. Several artists also embroidered words

A close look at B. J. Adams's machine-embroidered piece, "Order into Chaos," shows her style of carefully engineered rows of satin stitching that almost cover the surface. Adams works on an industrial sewing machine that stitches at high speed and has a wide range of widths on the zigzag setting used for the satin stitch.

Embellishing a quilt's surface by attaching beads and other non-textile objects was a common method of ornamenting Victorian crazy quilts and is increasingly popular among art quilters today. The contrast in texture, the added three-dimensional quality and the unexpected presence of a sometimes familiar object as part of the artful design of a quilt all combine to intrigue the viewer. Sometimes just a small touch of embellishment is included to add unexpected sparkle, such as the subtle beaded border in Jeanne Benson's Ten of Spades or the light frosting of bugle and seed beads that highlight adjacent areas of Patty Hawkins's two sympathetic Hearts. For other artists, embellishment is an important design technique and becomes part of the quilt's message.

A number of artists gave a prominent role to embellishment in their Full Deck quilts. Therese May, for example, playfully ornamented her childlike Queen of Clubs with paste jewels and safety pins and heavily dotted the surface with "beads" of thick paint. In the Ace of Spades, Jane Burch Cochran embellished her patchwork country scene with ornate patterns made with simple buttons, which along with gloves are a trademark of her work. Katharine Brainard's many embellishments in the Eight of Clubs help to make a wry comment on the

or phrases as part of their designs. Kathleen O'Connor, for example, embroidered the word "zero" to signify her Joker's numerical value. Jeanne Benson used her computerized sewing machine's alphabet capability to neatly embroider the phrase "A spade is a spade" along the winding stem of a vine in her Ten of Spades, while Joyce Marquess Carey painstakingly hand embroidered card-related phrases that take on ironic meanings as a backdrop for Lenin in her King of Clubs.

The embroidery technique of "couching," creating a continuous line by laying a decorative thread or cord on a fabric's surface and attaching it with stitches, was used by at least two artists in this collection. Dorothy Holden couched a long piece of passementerie cord that curls itself into a figure 5 to form a corner index for her Five of Diamonds. Deborah Anderson used the couching technique to add a silk floss outline to her Clubs.

role of women. Her fantastic mermaid has sequins for scales, swims in a sea of buttons and beads and wears a necklace of beads spelling out "Crazy Momma."

The embellishments of an art quilt often have symbolic meanings that relate to the quilt's content. Diane Herbort's King of Hearts is bejeweled with many tiny hearts, for example. Likewise, Lynne Sward's Queen of Diamonds is embellished with rhinestones to simulate a diamond's sparkle. Natasha Kempers-Cullen added numerous small charms and buttons in the shapes of farm animals, vegetables and other garden images, causing the abundance of her garden scene to virtually spill off the surface of her Seven of Spades. The identity of her card is communicated through seven miniature shovels stitched into the potting shed. To the African fabrics of her Nine of Spades, Carolyn Mazloomi added cowrie shells, once highly valued in Africa. To enhance their Joker's message of Earth healing, Susan Shie and James Acord included leather palms raised in peace and polymer clay crocodiles as protectors in keeping with their quilt's Native American imagery.

EDGE FINISHING
♦

A quilt maker eventually needs to give attention to the treatment of a quilt's edge, usually the last step in finishing off the "textile sandwich." The most common quilt finishing is a binding made of contrasting or harmonizing fabric. For an art quilter, even leaving the fabric edges raw can be a valid choice. In the Full Deck project the technique was left up to the individual artist, and therefore the edge treatment became another artistic decision.

The majority of artists chose to bind their quilts' edges, using fabric that coordinated somehow with the quilt top. Sometimes a solid color fabric or a print was used as a dramatic contrast for a quilt design, as in B. J. Adams's Seven of Diamonds, or to subtly blend with the quilt top, as in Kathleen Sharp's Nine of Hearts. Sometimes a fabric that was used in the quilt top was also used for the binding, as in Judy Becker's harmonious Four of Diamonds. Several artists, such as Pat Autenrieth and Joan Schulze, pieced their bindings in keeping with the piecework in their quilts, while some pieced their bindings to correspond with the color areas of their designs, as Diane Herbort and Marguerite Malwitz did. Other artists used fabrics that were similar in feeling or theme to the fabrics in their quilt tops, like Carolyn Mazloomi's African-inspired surface fabrics and binding. Artists who use surface design methods often used similar techniques both to create the quilt top and to decorate the binding, as did Lenore

Davis. Katherine McKearn finished her edges to the extent that she bound not only the outer edge of her quilt, but also the edges of the heart-shaped masks and their eye holes.

In several quilts, edges that had been bound were then embellished, such as with an inner edging of beads in the quilts of Jeanne Benson and Katharine Brainard or with decorative stitching as in Libby Lehman's Ace of Clubs. Jane Burch Cochran embellished the black binding of her Ace of Spades by dotting it with small white beads.

Some artists chose to add nothing extra to the edges of their quilts and instead merely presented a seamed edge using a pillowsliplike construction method. In this way, Linda MacDonald's Seven of Clubs retains its painterly quality and Michele Vernon's Ace of Diamonds preserves its uncluttered, geometric elegance. By contrast, Dorothy Holden's surface stitching just inside the seamed edge of her Five of Diamonds occasionally pulls the quilt's backing into view and reinforces the quilt's unsophisticated feeling. A number of artists brought prominence to the perimeters of their quilts by including a border in the design of their quilt top, a technique often used in traditional quilts, and then finished the actual edge unobtrusively by either seaming or binding.

A few artists dealt with their quilts' edges in ways that were quite individual. Deborah Anderson included a piping of cord in her quilt's edge seam. Jean Ray Laury used a whip stitch to overcast the cut edges of the two felt layers that act as her quilt's backing and also create its outermost edge. Joan Lintault appliquéd small clovers to a fabric perimeter, making the edge the only physically continuous element of her quilt.

WILD CARDS
♥

Art quilters, above all, make their own rules. They freely choose materials and techniques, combining and adapting them at will, and cross boundaries so often that it is sometimes fruitless to try to describe their quilts as fitting into any one category. Elizabeth Busch, for example, created a Queen of Hearts with a combination of commercial checks and stripes, her own elusively hand-painted broadcloth and heavier artist's canvas. She pieced together parts of the background with turned-under seam allowances and appliquéd other parts leaving fabric edges raw. She added imagery by drawing and painting directly onto the fabric and as well as by using a photo-transfer technique.

The uniqueness of many of the artists' individual techniques makes it difficult to give them a name. What would one call the metallic foil that several artists have added to the surface of their quilts? Is it an embell-

ishment, a surface design technique or perhaps another fabric? Are Chris Wolf Edmonds's wooden birds and Sandra Humberson's aluminum strips embellishments or appliqués?

But there is no real reason to try to pigeonhole anomalies like these. The viewer can simply enjoy the final effect and wonder at the skill and imagination of the artist. "Wild cards" such as some of the quilts in the Full Deck have come a long way from their traditional models, but they always retain the essential "textile sandwich" character of their forebears. Art quilts introduce a delightful new medium to the art world and present an updated version of the quilt that is ready to meet the twenty-first century.

the artists and their quilts

IN ALPHABETICAL ORDER BY ARTIST

b. j. adams

WASHINGTON, D.C.

Born 1931

The vibrant, complex wall pieces of **B. J. Adams** are well known in the corporate art world, where their expressions of precision and excitement appeal to engineers and bankers, as well as to many private collectors. The Seven of Diamonds was an ideal card choice to reflect the hard-edged, highly graphic technique that Adams has been using in some of her recent work.

Trained in both mathematics and art in college, Adams has always enjoyed puzzles and mazes. She likes to create design or technical problems and figure out how to solve them. Seeing an exhibition of Shoowa textiles from Zaire with their bold patterns of interlocking diamonds and diagonals led her to attempt similar effects in her own work, using an industrial sewing machine and her own intense color palette instead of nimble fingers and hand-dyed raffia.

The many-colored Diamonds on their reverberating backgrounds in her Seven of Diamonds are created entirely of machine embroidery. Using threads in gradations of color—and sometimes many colors—Adams has produced the sparkle of a natural diamond in a complicated design that continually tricks and delights the eye. An underlying multicolored patchwork shows through the narrow margins left between rows of stitching and creates shadows that add dimension to the geometric shapes. Only on

careful inspection is it apparent that the patchwork beneath each diamond contains the number seven, and that a large seven underlies the whole piece.

Adams finds inspiration for her designs in a variety of sources. She enjoys photographing the reflections in windows in order to study the distortion of line and shape, and she once based a whole series of pieces on the disorienting view of the world seen from the end of a bungee cord. The controversy over the canceling of the Mapplethorpe exhibit by the Corcoran Gallery in Washington, D.C., prompted her to create a group of "activist" artworks that dealt with the idea of censorship. In one way or another, her works are mirrors of our world.

Adams began her artistic career as a painter and sculptor. She has always liked exploring new ways to use materials, and early in her career she developed a series of three-dimensional pieces constructed of plastic tubing and employing basketry techniques. She began experimenting with fiber after seeing her first contemporary embroidery exhibit in 1961, and in the 1970s she switched to fiber completely. For a while she investigated every conceivable way of manipulating stripes. Her earlier interest in texture has given way to curiosity about line, movement and color. Her work continues to evolve

Shoowamaze, 1989. 43 x 49 in. Machine stitchery over striped fabrics. Photo by Breger & Associates.

as she generates endless new options for herself, posing design and technical problems and exploring multiple solutions in order to see what the results will be.

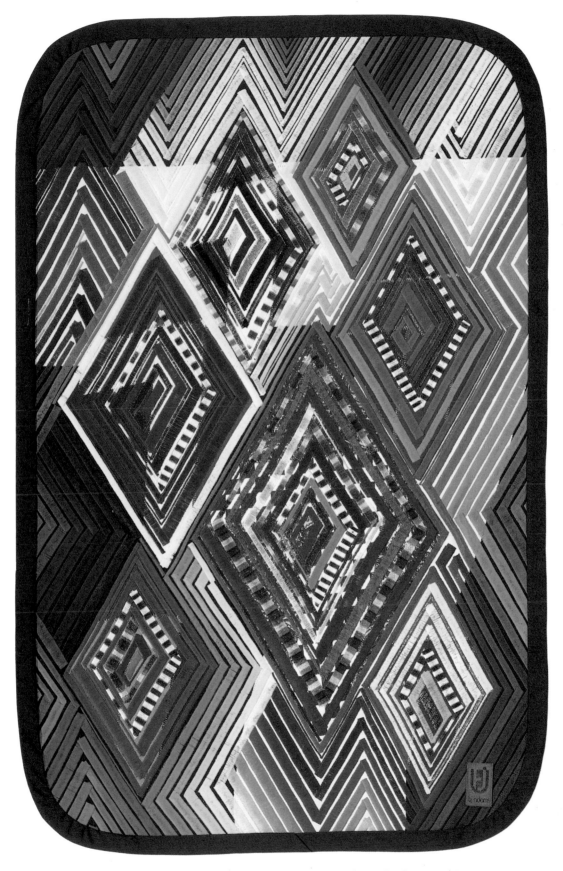

SEVEN OF DIAMONDS

Machine satin stitching over pieced and appliquéd fabrics. Cotton, linen, polyester and rayon fabrics; assorted threads.

deborAH
MeLtoN AnderfoN

C O L U M B U S ,   O H I O

....

Born 1937

Deborah Anderson studied drawing, painting and art history in college and went on to receive a master of arts in teaching from Harvard. Although her busy life did not immediately include an art career, she and her husband both admired antique textiles and built an extensive collection that includes 150 Oriental rugs, which fill trunks and cover the floors, walls and sometimes the ceilings of their home. "We are caretakers of these beautiful things for a short while." At an antique show in 1980 she bought some old quilt patches and soon began putting them together to make her first quilt.

Her first quilting class was with well-known quilter Nancy Crow. Anderson began working traditionally but moved on to "controlled innovation," a process in which she uses traditional techniques and designs as starting points but steps off to something new, constantly expanding her range of materials and techniques. She frequently has been inspired by patterns formed by old architectural elements, and most of her quilts deal with the past in some way.

A quilted banner that Anderson made for her church in the early 1970s led to a long series of liturgical commissions for Protestant, Catholic and Jewish congregations and institutions. Before beginning each of these, she asks religious or lay leaders of the congregation to talk about what emphasis they want in the banner

and then interprets their expression in fabric, form and color. "I'm not theologically trained; I'm just listening." She tries to design complex pieces that will hold the interest of frequent viewers. "I like things that make people look and look again."

Anderson's Nine of Clubs presents a complex surface that demonstrates her unique approach to design and construction. She began with a muslin base and thin batting and then added a pieced layer made up of hand-dyed cotton at top and bottom and irregularly tucked purple-black silkscreened sateen from Finland in the middle. She placed another layer of batting over everything to even up the surface made irregular by the tucks, and she topped off with a piece of French furnishing fabric with a swirl pattern, which ultimately became the Clubs. She formed the Club shapes through reverse appliqué by drawing her design on the quilt's back, stitching the design through all the layers, and then cutting away the negative spaces on the front to expose the tucked background. She zigzagged over the raw edges of the Clubs and then lightened the fabric with white pencil and repeated coats of thinned, white acrylic paint. She couched variegated hand-dyed silk floss over the edges of the Clubs and edged the quilt with rayon flanged cording.

Anderson chose the Nine of Clubs for its uneven number: "Symmetry

Structurally Unsound, 1990. 56 x 56 in. Appliqué, reverse appliqué, quilting. Photo by Kevin Fitzsimons.

is too comfortable; I like baroque designs that work." She also likes to design negative forms that are as interesting as the positive and include unanticipated details. The darker overlapped areas of the Clubs, formed by lightening them less than the main bodies of the Clubs, create the opposite effect of what would be expected when light-colored fabrics are overlapped. Likewise, light Clubs on a dark background are an unexpected contrast. Anderson's original idea for the card's imagery was to reflect trees on a grassy plain, but her Clubs could just as well be clover leaves in a field of grass. She drew her Club shapes too large to fit within the boundaries of her quilt so that they appear cut off, in emulation of the Oriental rug format that suggests, in the Islamic tradition, that a rug's border encloses a limited piece of infinite paradise.

NINE OF CLUBS

Machine appliqué and reverse appliqué, tucking, machine quilting. Cottons, sateen, silk threads, cotton and rayon cording, polyester batting.

patricia Autenrieth

HYATTSVILLE, MARYLAND

Born 1948

Patricia Autenrieth received formal training in sculpture, ceramics and printmaking while working on her B.F.A. at the Kansas City Art Institute, and since 1981 she has been teaching at the Corcoran School of Art in Washington, D.C. She is at home in the academic world of art and experienced in posing formal, focused studies of various subjects. In her own work, she is known for reproducing photographic images on paper and fabric through the use of rubbing, silkscreen printing, photo dyes and copy transfer. For her Queen of Spades she chose to do a fabric study of her mother, based on the only drawing of her that Autenrieth has ever done.

She has used this drawing as a theme in several watercolors but has never tried to reproduce it in fiber. After some practice, she was able to approximate the sketch by varying a zigzag stitch according to the thickness of the drawing line. She scribbled in the background shading lines on the organza overlay using fabric crayon. The quilting of the fabric sandwich was accomplished through the drawing lines and the machine embroidery used to create the Qs and some of the polka dots. She initially cut the fabric pieces larger than required to allow for shrinkage because of the excess quilting, but the quilt still ended up being too small and caused the left edge to curve in, roughly matching the curved line of the woman's back.

"I've done everything I can to compensate for the extra quilting without actually doing the piece over. I'm not that kind of artist—one who will alter her idea to fit the dimensions. I'm too satisfied with its expression." The woman in the drawing appears tired, or even asleep, or perhaps preoccupied with something. It is not apparent that she suffers from depression.

The somber, conservative fabrics that Autenrieth chose produce a sepia effect, which suggests the remembered past and which matches the mood of the piece. The lily-of-the-valley motifs in the organza overlay are reminiscent of the lily-of-the-valley perfume that her mother often wore, a tribute to the "lake" of those flowers that filled the yard of their home. The prize fabric in the quilt is the bronze taffeta of the Spade suitmarks, which came from scraps of a dress her mother made when Autenrieth was six and which she remembers her mother wearing in an Easter photograph of the family. "Oh, the power of fabric!"

The Queen of Spades was the card Autenrieth knew she wanted from the start, and she also knew she wanted to incorporate the drawing of her mother. She has many childhood memories of card playing and recalls that the Queen of Spades had particular significance in the game of Hearts. It suggested a dilemma that sometimes seemed real to her as a child:

Family photo from Easter 1954. Autenrieth is in the front row, left. Her mother wears a dress made from the bronze-colored taffeta that the artist later used in her Queen of Spades quilt. Photo by Karen Autenrieth.

"To win is to lose." As an artist, Autenrieth uses the visual to express emotions and memories that she finds impossible to put into words.

QUEEN OF SPADES

Hand appliqué; machine piecing, embroidery and quilting. Cottons, blends, taffeta, organza, polyester batting.

judy
becker

NEWTON, MASSACHUSETTS
....
Born 1939

When **Judy Becker** works in her studio, she listens to jazz. This is not surprising because quilting and jazz have much in common: they both are improvisational art forms, piecing together new identities out of improbable parts, and both are American inventions. She also used to play jazz piano.

In recent years, Becker has played around at developing a linear motif to use in repeating quilt blocks, her favorite patterning technique. The motif finally took shape as the number 4. (Coincidentally, "four" happened to be the position in the Modern Jazz Quartet series of "African Rhythms," the inspiration for the quilt she was working on at the time.) Her stylized "four block" turned out to be such an appealing and useful design that she went on to use variations of it in over twenty more quilts. It was an obvious choice for her to use again in interpreting the Four of Diamonds. Besides the number match, the Diamond's hard-edged angles echoed the motif's angularity, and its bright red color was in tune with her bold palette.

At first glance Becker's Four of Diamonds appears to be a cacophony of lines and shapes, but on closer study the viewer appreciates the precise rhythm and harmony of the piece. Her colors are very limited, but their high contrast and strength makes the quilt almost "jump off the wall," an effect that Becker strives for.

Her motifs also are very limited, to just fours and Diamonds. All of the yellow "four blocks" are identical, made with the same combination and placement of fabrics, differing only in orientation on the quilt. They are a familiar riff accompanying the major and minor red fours and Diamonds. The result is a true symmetrical double-headed playing card.

Becker started making quilts in 1972 after being inspired, like so many other artists, by the groundbreaking show at the Whitney Museum of American Art where quilts were exhibited for the first time as works of art. With two children and a full-time job as a teacher, she wasn't able to become a serious art quilter until 1981. Now she alternates between two or three different design techniques, always including elements that "touch back to the origins of quilting." The repetitive block is the most traditional design technique she uses and also the most frequent. Her quilts are sometimes pictorial, with "simple things" as their subjects, but more often they are boldly graphic and abstract. The inherent spontaneity of the medium is one of the qualities that attracted her to art quilting, just as it attracted her to jazz.

Anonymous Was a Woman, 1993.
47 x 62 in. Photo by David Caras.

FOUR OF DIAMONDS

"Poker Rag." Machine piecing, hand quilting. Cotton, chintz, cotton/polyester batting.

jeanne benson

COLUMBIA, MARYLAND

Born 1949

"Call a spade a spade" is the motto embroidered along the vine in **Jeanne Benson's** Ten of Spades, and it summarizes part of her design challenge with this card: to call things by their right names. Benson was immediately drawn to the suit of spades because of her identification of the suit-mark with a garden spade. For her it was an ideal image to use as the subject of a quilt because she often depicts items of daily life or stylizes flowers and plants to reflect her love of nature. However, she was in for a surprise when a visit to the library revealed that what she had been picturing as a garden spade was actually a short-handled trowel. But she liked the simple, functional beauty of the long-handled spade and decided to use it in her card design.

Her original idea was to have the trowel undergo a metamorphosis and become the Spade suitmark Escher-fashion, with the images fitting into each other. Faced with the long-handled spade, she decided to simplify the design but retain the mutation process, applying it both to the tools and to some vine leaves rambling up the center. The images mutate in both shape and color. Along the way they nearly take on the shapes of the other suits—diamond-shaped blades, three-lobed blades ornamented with clublike circles, heart-shaped red leaves—but in the end they evolve into their true suit identities and spades become Spades.

Benson trained as a graphic artist in college and went on to work for a sign

company, doing scale drawings and enlarging them to full size. She took up quilting in 1978 after being fascinated by sampler quilts and gravitated toward appliqué. This technique was more or less a fabric extension of her work for the sign company, where she carefully applied images and letters to a background. She went on to write a book, *The Art and Technique of Appliqué*, and teaches quilting and appliqué regularly at the Smithsonian. A design principle that she emphasizes to her students is to "define and simplify" their images. Benson learned the need for clear definition from her days as a sign maker. The need to simplify is dictated by the "needle-turn running stitch" technique she frequently uses for appliqué which leaves only an eighth of an inch for turning under at the edge and makes sharp angles difficult.

Many of Benson's own pieces draw on the quilting tradition of repeating the same image but incorporating subtle differences in each repetition, and the transformation of images in her Ten of Spades can be seen as an extension of this tradition. She likes to use symbolism when she can, so since the ten garden spades on the card matched her daughter's age, she added fourteen leaves to represent the age of her son also. For the quilting pattern she used a nine-patch design called "Card Trick." Although Benson usually prefers to appliqué by hand, she used a sewing machine for this piece in order to keep the quilt "very flat, graphic,

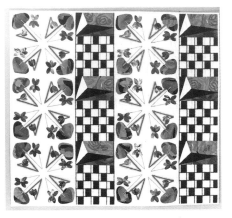

Featuring the Violets, 1992. 45 x 41½ in.

pristine." She also machine embroidered the writing on the vine. For the background material she chose coarse linen with its honest, almost burlap quality matching the earthy garden theme. To define the shape of the card and to "add a little sparkle to the ever-the-same, ever-so-plain Ten of Spades," she added a piping of beads just inside the card's border.

Benson most enjoys the design phase of quilting: setting up a problem, working through ideas and coming to a solution. Although her Ten of Spades incorporates many aspects of a traditional quilt—images in repetition, appliquéd designs against a solid background, familiar botanical subjects, a classic overall quilting pattern—and has a traditional playing card's virtue of being readable just as well upside down, the design and technical details and the interpretation of the card are uniquely her own, clearly demonstrating that she can call a Spade a Spade any way she wants.

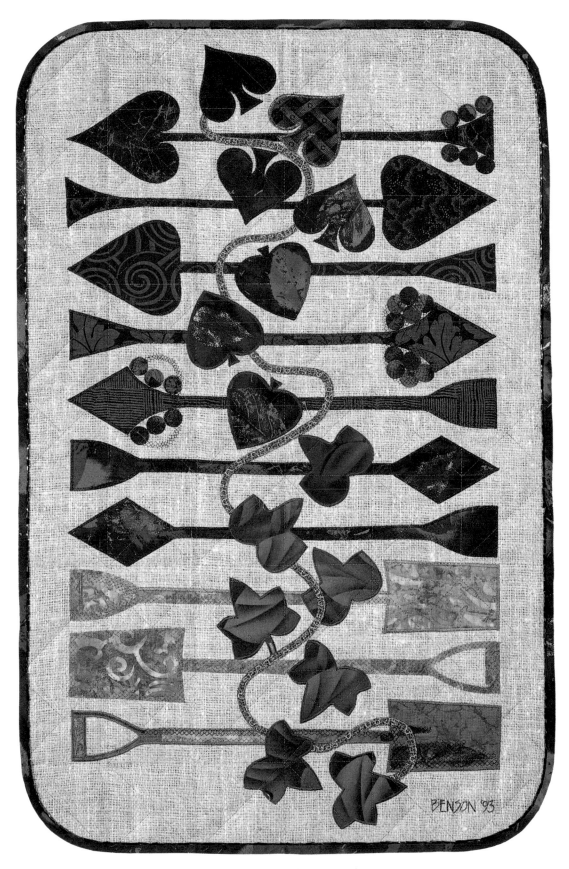

TEN OF SPADES
Machine appliqué, embroidery and quilting. Linen, cotton, beads, polyester batting.

KAREN felicity berkenfeld

NEW YORK, NEW YORK

Born 1943

Karen Berkenfeld had decided to use a baseball diamond for her card's suit-mark, and although she started with only a general knowledge of baseball lore, she soon learned that Jackie Robinson was the quintessential Jack of Diamonds. He was already twenty-eight years old when he started playing for the Brooklyn Dodgers in 1947, but he won major league baseball's first Rookie of the Year Award that year. This phenomenal second baseman went on to lead the National League in batting, stolen bases and double plays and was inducted into the Baseball Hall of Fame in 1962. He was also the first African American to play major league baseball.

Berkenfeld's playing card is also a baseball card, with multiple images like stop-action photos or like repeating quilt block motifs of Robinson—fielding a ball at the top, sliding into base at the bottom and batting in the middle. Creating this central figure taught Berkenfeld "Baseball Lesson #1: All batters do not bat alike." At first she could not find a good picture of Robinson in batting stance, so she tried borrowing the pose of another batter and sketching in Robinson's face. When she showed the drawing to her sports-fan husband, however, he immediately said, "That's Ted Williams!"

For the artwork on her Jack of Diamonds, Berkenfeld employed both stenciling and relief-printing techniques, which she has perfected to the

degree that the images look painted. She carved the action figures on blocks of adhesive-backed linoleum-like material, allowing her to mount the printing block on a transparent piece of Plexiglas so that she could see to position the image on the whole-cloth surface. Afterward she hand painted some of the details on the faces, such as the slight cast in one of Robinson's eyes. She also block printed the Brooklyn Dodger logo fabric, trying to give it the faded look of old uniform cloth. She stenciled the shapes of the baseball diamond, trees and scoreboard, and cut out letters to use as resists in order to show the teams' scores.

Berkenfeld's interest in printing developed in 1989–1990, after she had been quilting for about fifteen years and had become discouraged over the limitations of commercial fabrics. Printmaking showed her intriguing ways of creating images and patterns, and her previous subdued abstract quilts suddenly exploded with color and representational symbols. Since then she has acquired a printing press for her studio and has continued to study printing methods and art at various New York art schools. "When you study printmaking you never really finish." Berkenfeld recently received a grant from the Empire State Crafts Alliance to study nontoxic methods of printmaking on textiles.

Three Rivers, 1994. 53 x 48 in. Fabrics printed with collagraph and linoleum cuts. Photo by Karen Bell.

JACK OF DIAMONDS

Relief printing, stenciling, painting, machine piecing, hand quilting. Cotton, paint, wool batting.

katharine brainard

B E T H E S D A ,   M A R Y L A N D

....

Born 1956

Moment of Impact, 1992. 46 x 31 in. Based on the split second of realization before impact in a car accident and the resultant feeling of loss of control and impending chaos.

Katharine Brainard's quilts deal with life's challenges and rewards. Some of her subjects are lighthearted and celebrate "the mess and stuff of life" found on a refrigerator door or bathroom floor. Others deal with darker universal themes and confront difficult emotions such as the terror of childhood nightmares or the desperation of suicide. In the tradition of making quilts to record family events, she looks at her life with both poignancy and humor. "We patch together our own lives day to day, one piece at a time. We are each a work of art."

Brainard's Eight of Clubs is an adult fantasy that celebrates a special figure from the fairy tales of her childhood. For her, a mermaid was something to aspire to be, and this quilt is "about hanging on to dreams instead of letting go of them when you grow up." She included the simple materials of childhood in constructing her fantasy image: giant rickrack to suggest ocean waves and the mermaid's golden hair; buttons for bubbles in the water and plastic beads for the mermaid's necklace, spelling out "crazy momma." The free-form Club shapes swimming in the background might be little mermaid embryos waiting for their own fingers and fins to emerge. As a legend at the bottom of her quilt, Brainard has embroidered the pronouncement of Simone de Beauvoir: "One is not born a woman, one becomes one."

As an art major in college, Brainard first distinguished herself as a graffiti artist, being expelled at one point for painting partying monsters on the dormitory walls at night. She discovered, however, that she could do similar artwork as murals for class assignments and channeled her vandalism energy into a more socially acceptable form. After graduation she went on to earn an additional A.A. in advertising and graphic design. Her use of fiber as an art medium coincided with motherhood: "Once I started having children I just naturally went to quilting. It seemed to be the form that could handle what I wanted to do visually." The direction of her work was influenced, ironically, by the rigidity of the clerk from whom she bought her first quilting materials, who insisted that a quilt had to be made in a certain way and with certain fabrics. Brainard's rebellious nature prompted her to look for new techniques at any cost!

The quilting that she does today is very spontaneous, a "process of letting go, accepting what is happening in the artwork, rather than trying to control it." She describes her style as influenced by whatever she's seen most recently: primitive art, Picasso, Keith Haring or her children's cartoons. Frequently her quilts explore emotions, such as her best-known piece, "Divorce Quilt," a cathartic, healing piece she made mostly "during two exhausting weeks" before the final dissolution of her ten-

year marriage. The quilt's unconventional subject matter and its humor and honesty brought it widespread attention and led to numerous television and radio interviews with the artist.

Another side of Brainard's quilting, and one that is very important to her, involves her collaborative efforts with children. She tries to make a quilt each year together with each of her three children's classes. In this modern approach to the quilting bee, the children sometimes create and cut out shapes for appliqué, or Brainard may machine embroider over their magic marker drawings. These school projects have led to other commissions, most notably one to create twenty-two quilts for the new Korean War Memorial in collaboration with children of participating nations. Brainard has begun to receive increased media coverage for her quilts done with children, instead of primarily for those with traumatic subjects like suicide or divorce, and she welcomes this as a positive development.

Brainard 1993

CRAZY MOMMA

ONE IS NOT BORN
A WOMAN,
ONE BECOMES ONE.

EIGHT OF CLUBS

Machine appliqué, embroidery and quilting; hand embellishment. Cotton, satin, trims, sequins, beads, buttons, cotton batting.

SARA brOWN

SILVER SPRING, MARYLAND
....
Born 1933

As with many artists, **Sara Brown's** work is a response to the world around her, and her world has been very large. As a result of her husband's job as a correspondent with the Voice of America, she has lived in a number of different countries and has become increasingly sensitized to "the sense-less killing and suffering going on in so many corners of the world."

A theme for Brown's Four of Spades came from a line of poetry by William Cowper (1731–1800): "And spades the emblems of untimely graves." She interprets this line by referencing tragic trouble spots of the world and by incorporating the elements that she uses in many of her fabric assemblages: combinations of hand-dyed and commercial fabrics, household articles like buttons and lace used in new ways and a variety of surface design techniques. Her Spade suitmarks are all pointing downward as if digging graves, or perhaps they are bombs flying down to bury whole villages. Her 4s march inexorably on in a stark, desolate line.

Some of the fabrics that Brown used for the background and border of the quilt are pieces that she either collected abroad or dyed herself. Some she batiked with the line from Cowper's poem. Other fragments of cloth announce the names of troubled places in the world and are attached to the quilt as if posted on a wall. Many of the fabrics she included have frayed edges, suggesting that the violence is unfinished. For her palette she used grayed versions of the primary colors, with the exception of the bright blood red. She thinks of the buttons in this piece as "markers" ticking off troubled places or as the gravestones that aren't erected. These buttons are the workaday kind used on the clothing of everyday people, who are usually the victims.

Brown's artistic sensibilities were formed when she lived in Japan and earned a master's certificate in the Sogetsu discipline of ikebana. Although its focus was flower arranging, she learned principles of line, color and simplicity of detail that have strongly influenced her work in mixed media. Her subject is often memory and lately has reflected her concern with social issues. Out of the "frustrations and inability to do anything constructive" about ethnic cleansing in Bosnia, communal riots in India and the emaci-ated bodies of Somali children paraded nightly on television news, she decided to use her Four of Spades "as a kind of testimony to the innocents of the world, as an indictment of those of us who perpetuate these injustices if only by our inaction."

Female Grid Number 2 (detail), 1990.
Mixed media (wood, cloth, lace, buttons).

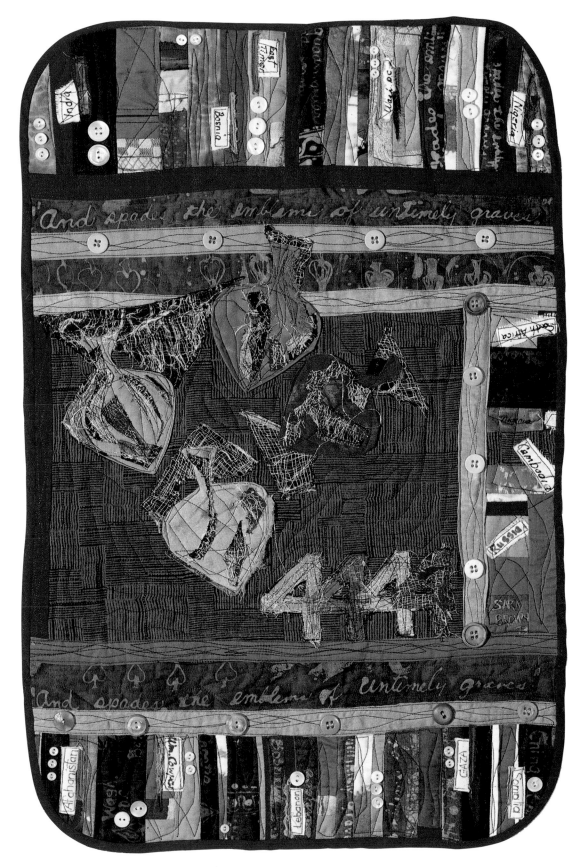

FOUR OF SPADES

"And Spades the Emblems of Untimely Graves." Batik, machine piecing, appliqué, hand embroidery, embellishment.
Cottons, netting, hand-dyed fabric, buttons, flannel batting.

tAfi broWN

Tafi Brown makes quilts about things that are important in her life. "Our lifestyles and our art influence each other, and as artists we have to be aware of and take advantage of that." All of her work includes blue color photo prints that reflect her longtime interest in photography and the cyanotype process in particular. Her imagery comes from the subject matter of her daily life, often the wood beams of house construction or the pine boughs and wildflowers of rural New Hampshire where she lives.

Brown received a B.F.A. in art education and an M.F.A. in ceramics from Pratt Institute and has taught various aspects of art at every level from elementary school to college. She first became interested in cyanotype printing when she attended a photography symposium with the idea of learning how to put photographs on ceramics, but while she was there she wandered into a workshop on printing with cyanotype on fabric. She soon appreciated the possibilities and unique effect of this process and turned from ceramics to cyanotype pieced quilts as her means of expression.

Since cyanotype is synonymous with "blueprint," this imagery technique also coincided with Brown's interest in architecture. She had thought of being an architect when she was young and during the 1980s worked for a company that designed timber-frame houses, first doing

drafting and photography and then actual designing. In the first quilts she made, she included cyanotype images from house construction. Brown uses photographs as modular design units and manipulates them so that viewers are not immediately aware that they are looking at photographs. She often includes rhythmic mirror-image patterns and encourages dualities and visual ambiguities that suggest hidden meanings. Although the restrictions of cyanotype's blues limit her possibilities somewhat, she finds that there are still infinite problem-solving challenges within the medium. She does all her own photographic and darkroom work and uses the same chemical formula for cyanotype processing that was developed by Sir John Herschel in 1842, which she prefers over modern methods because of the original formula's superiority in print clarity, permanency and safety.

In her Two of Spades, Brown included some multicolored fabric that she had airbrushed specifically to coordinate with her characteristic blues, but mostly she used fabric printed as cyanotypes in the form of both photographs and "photograms," which are produced without a camera. She created the images of white pine branches by using the photogram process, placing the branches against sensitized white cotton fabric and using sunshine as a light source. The branch and the pine needles blocked

Beam Team, 1992. 54 x 53 in. Fabrics printed through cyanotype process are used throughout this quilt.

the sun's rays and cast shadows against the fabric. After the fabric was rinsed in water, the area that had been exposed to sunlight turned blue but the shadows remained white. Because of the photogram process, the white pine branches are necessarily life size; but there was no such limitation on the cyanotype chickens, which were photographs and therefore reproducible in any size. Brown used chickens because she once raised them and likes them a lot, and their shapes fit conveniently into the curves of the Spades. The juxtaposition of chickens and pine trees and their out-of-scale size relationship gives a surrealistic quality to her Two of Spades. But as she points out, "Playing cards are surreal to begin with."

TWO OF SPADES

Cyanotype photograms; airbrushing; machine appliqué, embroidery and quilting. Cotton, rayon embroidery thread, felt batting.

eLizabetH A. buƒcH

B A N G O R ,   M A I N E

....

Born 1943

Elizabeth Busch began as a painter, studying for a B.F.A. in both painting and art education at the Rhode Island School of Design. For the next twenty years or so, she worked as an art instructor and as an architectural interior designer, with painting continuing to be her artistic medium of choice. When her children were small she enjoyed working with colorful cloth to make toys for them and soon began to see potential in combining purchased fabric and painted canvas. Since 1987 she has been a full-time studio artist, creating art quilts that are extensions of her painting.

Contrast has always been an important principle in Busch's art, whether in materials, colors, methods, ideas or attitudes. For example, she often combines lightweight purchased or dye-painted cotton fabrics with heavier artist's canvas that she paints with acrylics. Also, her painted cloudlike images contrast with the pieced grid structure and geometric patterns reminiscent of her architectural renderings. "I create spatial ambiguities to put the viewer in different places at the same time—inside and outside, awake and dreaming." She sees "inside" and "outside" as "two partners on a path" in her painted and pieced quilts. Purchased fabrics represent the outside world and are there to provide a contrast "to the fluid, impressionistic values and textures of the painted colors." Busch frequently

juxtaposes the representational and the abstract, which satisfies her need for both styles. The last steps in the process, hand quilting and embroidery, allow her "to become physically reacquainted with a piece created at arm's length on the wall."

In creating the Queen of Hearts, Busch has characteristically used contrasting and innovative materials and techniques. She cut the Q and the Heart suitmark from acetate gel, such as that used for filters to give color to stage lights, and coated the shapes with metal leaf. She pieced the quilt's surface from commercial prints, dye-painted pima cotton and acrylic-painted unsized artist's canvas. The sentimental pictures that she included in the center of the quilt are contrasted by the harsh method she used to reproduce them: she rubbed dry-cleaning fluid onto the backs of the photocopies, instantly transferring the images to the fabric on which the photocopies had been placed. Busch explains that this process is very quick and the result is washfast, but it is far from ideal. The copy is not always clear, which for her is an attraction because it adds to the dreamlike quality that she favors. But also, the dry-cleaning fluid gives off "nasty fumes."

In representing the figure of the Queen of Hearts, Busch departed from the image of the Queen on real playing cards, which to her looked "cold, domineering, menacing." In Busch's

This Old House, 1993. 68 x 63 in. Photo by Dennis Griggs.

mind the Queen of Hearts would be gentle, a "Queen of Love and Kindness, soft and strong at the same time, the Essence of Life and Spirit." The pastel drawing at the top of the piece is how she thinks a benevolent Queen of Hearts would look. In Busch's own life, she saw these tender feelings as central to the relationship between herself and her children. She therefore chose to make this idea central to her quilt and to portray it literally, as she says, "with photocopy transfers of me as a little girl and my children, Kim and David, sprouting from that childlike place within me that enables creativity."

QUEEN OF HEARTS

Hand painting, drawing and embroidery; photo transfer; machine appliqué, piecing and quilting.

Cotton canvas, blend fabrics, Mylar, metal leaf, polyester batting.

joyce
Marquess Carey

MADISON, WISCONSIN

....

Born 1936

Computer-generated drawing for the King of Clubs.

As an artist, **Joyce Carey** is primarily known for her extremely large art quilts designed as site-specific commissions for professional and residential settings. They usually are based on geometric designs and are stitched together from small pieces of luxurious fabrics in rich, bright colors. They challenge the viewer with their three-dimensional appearance. These commissions are how she makes her living and are what she works on Monday through Friday. On weekends she makes quilts for fun.

A recent series of her "fun quilts" resulted from the discovery in 1989 of a large quantity of Jacquard-woven silk banners made in China, each emblazoned with the face of a Communist leader. She bought all she could find and since then has enjoyed integrating them into art quilts in various ways. Not doing any fabric printing herself, she was happy to find material with subject matter already on it. The timing of the find was providential, too, because 1989 was the year the Berlin Wall fell and communism began falling apart all over the world, providing a wealth of opportunity for politically inspired artwork.

The idea of interpreting a playing card appealed to Carey immediately because she saw it as "a good opportunity to use one of my Communists." She wanted to create a King to represent a totalitarian "King" of the USSR, and she chose Lenin for the role since he had led the Bolshevik Revolution in 1917 and had helped turn the idealistic Communist Manifesto into a nightmare. (Stalin would have been an excellent candidate, too, but Carey had used up all her Stalins.) A Communist king would be a red king, of course, "but the red card suits are too sweet." The black ones were more menacing, and the clubs, particularly, evoked thoughts of killing and terrorizing. So she chose the King of Clubs, who became a "Red King in a Black Suit." "Once I get a title, the rest is easy."

A motorcycle jacket was a natural for Lenin's black suit, "ominous and definitely very black." She studied jackets pictured in cycling magazines and on young men riding the New York subway. In shopping for material, she looked for leatherlike fabrics and found that heavy satin was just right. The woven silk Lenin face turned out to be too large so she had an iron-on transfer made to size. She used Painter and Canvas programs on her Macintosh Quadra 700 computer for design and layout and drew images of St. Basil's Cathedral, an immediately recognizable symbol of Russia, and typed in as many phrases as she could think of that related to cards. She loves "words, puns, double meanings" so was "delighted to find that so many card phrases could easily refer to a corrupt Communist government."

The finished piece is a combination of appliqué and both hand and machine embroidery. She used cross-stitch to create the corner indices identifying the card and hand embroidered all the card phrases, which "took thousands of hours." St. Basil's is part machine embroidery and part appliqué. Carey's fondness for three-dimensional effects can be seen in Lenin's jacket collar and lapels that fold out from the surface and in the zippers that really zip.

Carey received her arts training during work on her three university degrees, including a master of fine arts. Her fiber interests led from knitting to weaving and finally to art quilting, a medium that allowed her to finish large pieces in a reasonable amount of time. She began a teaching career as a lecturer at the University of Wisconsin in 1973 and worked up to full professor of textile design in 1988. The next year she resigned from the university in order to concentrate on her art and has been working full-time in her studio ever since.

KING OF CLUBS

"Red King in a Black Suit." Photo transfer on silk, hand and machine appliqué and embroidery, machine quilting.

Silk, polyester, satin, embroidery floss, zippers, studs.

jANe burch cochrAN

R A B B I T   H A S H ,   K E N T U C K Y

....
Born 1943

Jane Burch Cochran always knew she wanted to be an artist, from the time she and her grandmother Berkeley Burch used to gather flowers and carefully arrange them and then paint watercolors of their arrangements. After college she worked at a succession of statistical jobs for which her mathematics major had prepared her, but she also studied painting at the Cincinnati Art Academy. A growing hobby of collecting beads led to a full-time costume jewelry business during the 1970s. A fondness for recycling materials from other eras eventually directed her to fiber collage, in which she could "combine the loose, free feeling of abstract painting with the time-consuming and controlled techniques of beading and sewing."

Today Cochran is a full-time artist who makes large, exuberant art quilts, combining painted backgrounds, classic piecing patterns and embellishments drawn from her own collection of beads and from flea-market finds. She often includes buttons and fabric from old clothing or other discarded items and thinks that they add "a mystical quality" that comes from the essence of the former owner or the former life of the object.

"I like the viewer to make up his or her own narrative about my work while I furnish the characters." Her "characters" are rarely human figures but rather familiar objects that become focal points and take on symbolic significance. The characters in the Ace of Spades are two gloves, a white one clutching the handle of the spade and a black one almost hidden in the blackness of the spade itself. Three baby-block cubes from an old quilt tumble across the surface and satin leaves sprout from sequin stems.

Cochran added other details out of whimsy: the red buttons like bright fingernail polish on the fingers of both gloves; the button pattern on the white glove forming a scarlet letter A for "Ace;" the green thumb produced by being dipped into green opalescent ink. Cochran likes the lacy effect of the white pearl buttons against the black spade. It reminds her of the white pattern on the Ace of Spades suitmark in an actual deck of cards harking back to a 1765 law in England that required the tax stamp to be printed on the Ace of Spades. She also included some unique structural techniques: quilting with a mixture of long stitches and cross-stitches and appliquéing with bugle beads.

Cochran does have her own ideas about the symbolism of her images, however. "I use hands for 'reaching,' 'searching,'" and gloves in different colors suggest people of different races. Her Spade is a garden tool meant for digging, and digging produces growth, hence the leaves growing from the patchwork ground.

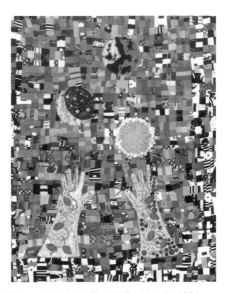

When All Is As It Should Be (detail), 1991. Photo by Pam Monfort.

"What I see in this Ace of Spades is me (the white woman) reaching and digging to grow" and in a larger sense "the different races reaching to each other to grow and be friends."

ACE OF SPADES

Machine piecing, hand appliqué using beads, hand quilting with large stitches and cross-stitch. Various fabrics, gloves, beads, buttons, sequins, paint, old Baby Block quilt pieces, manufactured fabric leaves, cotton/polyester batting.

dee DANLey-brOwN

PARADISE, CALIFORNIA

Born 1937

Dee Danley-Brown is a California native who in 1982 found herself transplanted to New York City. The drastic change in the ambiance and the architecture of her environment affected both the medium and the message of her art. A professional potter while living in California, she switched to fiber when she moved east since it had always held an attraction for her and seemed more practical in her new urban setting. The Amish Quilt exhibit then at the Folk Art Museum helped to direct her interest to quilting, and she went on to become one of the founders of the New York Art Quilt Network.

Although she began by copying traditional quilting patterns, Danley-Brown "started fooling around with changing things very early." She saw similarities between the repeated geometric forms of quilt blocks and the city blocks and buildings around her and began to concentrate on architectural themes in her imagery. The immense skyscrapers and the frenzied life of the city led her to examine how buildings fit into their surroundings and how people view them. She plays with different perspectives and includes views of buildings from a variety of angles in one piece. Her quilt construction remains rooted in the traditional techniques of piecing and appliqué, but she takes artistic liberties such as padding individual

buildings and only partially stitching them down to give a bas relief effect.

When Danley-Brown was assigned the Three of Clubs, she knew immediately that her clubs were going to be the kind that people "go to." "The Old Boy Network in New York is so overt compared to California. In the East it seems so important what you belong to, who you know, where you went to school." The club suitmarks on her card are brilliant emblems that sit atop three businessmen's clubs, as if marking shrines. The sidewalks converging in a vanishing point are trod by beetle-like businessmen, little wind-up toys waddling to their sanctuaries.

After she moved to New York, Danley-Brown found herself collecting black-and-white fabrics and finally realized that it was because the city had almost no color. Its overwhelming impression was monochromatic gray, echoed in the dull tones of businessmen's suits. Accordingly, she used black, white and shades of gray almost exclusively for her Three of Clubs. The only colors are the faint yellow glow coming from some of the windows of the club buildings, to indicate the lights are still on inside, and the red and fuchsia highlights that Danley-Brown permits as punctuation for the piece, just as businessmen are allowed a little color in their neckties.

Metropolitan Postcard, 1989. 49 x 61 in.

THREE OF CLUBS

Machine and hand piecing, appliqué, machine quilting. Cotton, cotton/polyester batting.

Ardyth Davis

RESTON, VIRGINIA

Born 1930

Ardyth Davis does not consider herself a quilter, although she has been making quilts since the late 1970s. Rather, she is a fiber artist who explores the possibilities of the fiber medium's many manifestations, of which quilting is only one. Her interest as an artist is in color and texture and how fiber can be manipulated to reflect the beautiful and subtle textures of the natural landscape.

Most recently, Davis has been influenced by the high peaks of the Colorado Rockies, and she has created several fabric collages using pleated silk to suggest the ridged nature of rocks and mountains, whose many layers are built up over millions of years. For the Full Deck she chose the King of Diamonds to interpret, not for its value as a face card but for the design possibilities in the letter K. In its angularity she saw fragments of a Diamond's shape and also the sharp peaks she had been depicting in her mountain series. In addition, the playing card's royalty would be well suited by the richness of her pleated silk and metallic threads. Her design ideas solidified when research into diamonds and kings' crowns revealed a similarity of shape between a pear-shaped cut diamond and the cone-shaped crown worn by early Russian czars.

The complex surface of Davis's King of Diamonds is the combined product of several processes, just as many elements combine to create geologic formations. She created the ripple effect in the large purple-green and red areas by using a smocking pleater to form ridges in pieces of silk and silk organza, which she then painted with dyes and layered over other pieces of painted silk. She brings out the multi-layer nature of the piece by sometimes pleating the underlying fabric in an opposing direction or by sandwiching metallic ribbon between the layers of silk. She simulates the appearance of brushed gold on areas of the surface through color washes and by embellishing with chain-stitch embroidery using metallic thread.

Davis topped her king's cone-shaped crown with a traditional "jewel" that she fashioned from a metal bead cap and metallic thread. When the quilt was finished, she "realized there was also an upside-down crown sitting on top of the Russian crown," which gave her playing card a nominal double-headed quality. The forward edge of her K nestles against a partial Diamond. Davis does not use actual imagery in her work, and, accordingly, she includes no clear representations of actual playing card symbols in this piece. Instead, one could say that her abstract King of Diamonds is made up of symbols of symbols.

Ardyth Davis works with a smocking machine to gather silk fabric into small pleats.

KING OF DIAMONDS

"Peak II / Violet." Pleating, shibori (tied resist dyeing), painting, appliqué, hand embroidery and quilting.
Silk, metallic ribbon, cotton, silk and metallic threads, metal embellishment.

LeNore daViS

NEWPORT, KENTUCKY

Born 1936

For **Lenore Davis**, design has been a lifelong interest and also an occupation: she is an object maker. With an undergraduate major in drawing, painting and design and an M.F.A. in ceramics, she was prepared to work in both two and three dimensions. She began working in fiber in 1969, first creating soft sculpture figures and then art quilts. She is a former board member and president of the Surface Design Association and has taught workshops and been a full-time fiber artist for over twenty years. Her work continues to evolve as she discovers new tools and as doors open to new ideas.

Cotton velveteen is a material that Davis discovered early on and liked immediately. The plush texture of the pile gives warmth and depth to a surface, and applied color combines with the nap to produce a sensuous chatoyant quality, a directional luster that changes when viewed from different angles. She has used velveteen in both her three-dimensional figures and her quilts.

Davis constructs all of her quilts from whole cloth, although the block-printing technique she has been using recently emulates traditional pieced block patterning.

She creates her designs using textile paints and fiber reactive dyes, which penetrate the cotton fibers of the velveteen's pile. Several years ago she started printing with monotype techniques and building pictures and patterns out of many small design blocks. Her procedure is to sponge paint onto the flat rubber surface of a small square or rectangular block, draw a design in the wet paint and then print on the velveteen surface using the pressure of her hand. She then wipes off the block, sponges it with paint again and draws the next design. She generally prints in black, and after the textile paint has been heat-set and cured, she adds color using fiber reactive dyes applied with a paint brush.

Davis used her characteristic techniques of printing and painting on velveteen to produce a Four of Hearts that is a warm, sensuous valentine. The intricate arrangement of small printed units suggests a hand-pieced quilt, although the modular designs have been block printed on whole cloth. Davis created a feeling of movement by adding various wavy and directional lines to move the eye. She used a stencil to paint the four large hearts in the corners and introduced a grid pattern into two of them by placing a textural grid beneath the cloth and using a rubbing technique to transfer the pattern. She also used the technique of rubbing, called *frottage*, to create other textural effects in the red background. For the quilting, she hand stitched the whole piece with

The Yellow Diamond, 1994. 60 x 60 in. Whole cloth using monotype printing and hand painting. Cotton velveteen, paint, dye, metallic thread.

a tailor's long zigzag "collar stitch," using a black-and-gold metallic thread that adds a glaze to the quilt's surface.

A recent design influence on Davis's quilts has come from Oriental rugs, stemming from some repair work she has been doing for a Cincinnati rug dealer. She has been "into red," for example, and the plush of the velveteen she uses mimics the pile of a knotted carpet. Her Four of Hearts, with its rich color, central medallion and symmetrical organization of small units and symbols, might actually be viewed as a miniature Oriental carpet.

FOUR OF HEARTS

Whole cloth with monotype printing, painting, hand quilting. Cotton velveteen, textile paint, dye, metallic thread, polyester batting.

chris Wolf edmonds

LAWRENCE, KANSAS

....

Born 1943

Chris Edmonds is a multitalented artist whose work is constantly evolving. She began making traditional pieced quilts in 1965 and progressed from a needlework hobbyist "trying to make something pretty to decorate the house" to a serious art quilter. Along the way she has figured out how to combine quilting with her skills in painting, printmaking and woodworking.

For the Five of Clubs, Edmonds pieced a background from alternating strips of her hand-painted fabric, sections of strip-piecing and a commercial black-and-white stripe. She printed the spiral patterns and the border color bars using woodblocks that she had carved, painted the fringe for the spirals and added a background 5 with a brush-dabbing process. She hand cut the wooden ravens and appliquéd them to the surface of the quilt with brass wire.

A fifth-generation Kansan, Edmonds lives on an eighty-acre farm where she and her investment broker husband raise Christmas trees and American paint horses. Living close to the land, she is motivated to preserve the color and spirit of the world around her. "Everything I do relates to nature and the process of life." The color inspiration for her Five of Clubs sprang from the time of its construction. "It was late winter. The color in the fields and woods was still a mix of deep grays and browns, but the wet warmer weather had filled them with

the muted lacy magenta of red bud trees and 'purple forest.' It was a time of renewal in the spiral of life, and as I watched a flock of blackbirds perched in the bare branches of the button-wood tree, I was reminded that 'spring begins with winter and death begins with birth.'"

Edmonds learned her needle skills from her mother and grandmother and also pursued interests in painting and printmaking. These were merely avocations, however; her bachelor of science degree from the University of Kansas was in speech and hearing education, and she went on to teach in public schools for several years. When she lived in California in the 1970s, she began selling her prints at fairs and through galleries and started designing her own quilts. Their success made her realize that she could make art a career. She became known for the photographic effect of her appliquéd "picture" quilts in which she translated pictorial subjects into fabric. She began receiving commissions from major corporations and is the author of two pattern books based on her own quilt designs.

Edmonds's later quilts have arisen from relatively simple design concepts and have dealt with "illusory space, form, light and motion." They often make use of the repeating-block tradition of quilting, but all are based on her original designs and employ striking use of color. Most recently

she has been drawing on woodworking skills learned from her father. "He did incredible inlaid three-dimensional birds, with no stain, just the wood." Edmonds has her own woodworking shop where she carves animals and blocks for printing and makes furniture. After her father died in 1991 she inherited his woodworking tools and has been experimenting with ways to incorporate the hard edges of wood in the soft, flexible medium of a quilt.

FIVE OF CLUBS

Hand painting and printing on cotton, appliqué with hand-cut and painted wood appliqués, machine piecing and quilting.

Cotton, wood, brass wire.

SUSAN
bALL fAeder

NEW YORK, NEW YORK

Born 1952

Star of Fortitude, 1991. 64 x 64 in. Machine piecing and hand quilting. Japanese cottons and Thai silks. Photo by Fred Slavin.

Susan Faeder's Six of Diamonds grew out of a game of solitaire. Recuperating in bed after a bad case of pneumonia in early 1993, she often welcomed the company of playing cards to pass the time. Late one night she found herself staring at the Six of Diamonds, attracted by its orderliness and the spaces between the suitmarks. When she squinted her eyes, the concave sides of the Diamond shapes seemed to outline the traditional Double Wedding Ring quilting pattern. She had previously been invited to participate in the Full Deck project but had declined because of the press of other commitments, but suddenly the Six of Diamonds seemed to be a good omen, so she asked if she could change her mind and make this card.

Faeder wanted her Six of Diamonds to be readily identifiable, so she designed a simple cross arrangement of six suitmarks, represented by the familiar jewel shape of a cut diamond. She was additionally attracted to the gemstone image because of her interest in Middle Earth and the healing power of crystals. She pieced the diamonds on her quilt from triangles of commercial and hand-dyed fabrics, and she added a sheer overlay over some of them to further the illusion of light and depth. For the background she used cotton fabric with a moiré print that gives a watery, flowing feeling. She quilted the purple background with metallic thread, in angular lines

to reflect the diamonds' facets and in concentric rings to connect the four center stones. The resulting imagery of her Six of Diamonds contains no reference to the Double Wedding Ring pattern that was her original inspiration but instead suggests the solitaire diamond of an engagement ring.

As is often the case, Faeder came to her quilting career in a roundabout way. The focus of her college studies and subsequent work had been Japan, since she had become fascinated with Japanese culture as a high school exchange student. She lived in Japan, became fluent in the language and at various points worked in a Japanese department store, travel agency and antique business. She took up quilting when she became pregnant, choosing to stay at home and "touch beautiful things" instead of deal with the high-strung world of antiques. Some of the quilts she went on to make were strongly based on traditional patterns, while others were like collages with free-form abstractions, but they all had in common the process of self-discovery for the artist.

Several years later, when Faeder was working in a New York quilt shop, a well-known Japanese quilt *sensei* (master) and a Japanese quilt shop owner came into the store to buy material. Coincidentally, Faeder had met the sensei, Shizuko Kuroha, in Japan and ended up selling the two quilters enough fabric to stock three

shops. Through them she also learned of a quilt festival that was soon to take place in Japan, so she decided to quit her job, cash in her savings account and go to the festival. The quilting she saw there and her research confirmed her belief that quilt making is more popular in Japan than anywhere outside the United States.

This experience led her to present a number of lectures on American quilting for the Japanese and on Japanese quilting for Americans. In 1988 Faeder inaugurated her own business, "Quilters' Express To Japan," for the purpose of organizing and leading tours for adventurous quilters from around the world who wanted to visit Japan. She has since expanded and has begun importing Japanese fabrics and specialty items that she sells at quilt festivals, through a mail order catalog and by appointment at her Greenwich Village workshop. She has adopted the Japanese word *Kakehashi* to describe her role in this "mysterious affair" she has had with Japan. The word suggests that a person has become a bridge; in Faeder's case she is a bridge between the cultures and the quilters of two countries.

SIX OF DIAMONDS

Machine piecing, hand appliqué and quilting. Cotton, polyester, metallic thread, cotton batting.

caryL
bryer faLLert

O S W E G O ,   I L L I N O I S

....

Born 1947

A **Caryl Bryer Fallert** quilt is a color and light show with intriguing complexities. Her combinations of color progressions and manipulated fabrics produce an effect of energy, either coming from within or moving across the surface. Whether in bold organic designs inspired by Georgia O'Keeffe or geometric patterns that "dance off the walls," the vitality of her work energizes the viewer.

Fallert's three-dimensional Three of Diamonds illustrates a technique that she has used often. She began the quilt by piecing a background and then cutting it into strips. When reassembling the strips, she inserted two-sided "tucks" that she had prepared from two different sets of fabrics. In this case, she cut one side from black-and-white striped material and the other from fabrics that she had hand dyed in gradations of light-to-dark gray. The final quilting secures a twist in the tucks that produces an illusion of movement and light across the surface.

Although Fallert most often works in a vibrant array of colors, she limited her palette to neutrals for the background of the Three of Diamonds. The contrast of the red Diamond suitmarks emphasizes the card's simplicity and brings out the subtleties of the shades of background gray. The bandanna-print border on this quilt is also somewhat atypical of her work because she generally uses hand-dyed solid-color fabrics rather than prints. However, the bandanna's workaday association suggests the democratic human connection to cards, and its familiar print recalls the ornate red or blue designs that cover the backs of poker decks. The two-sided tucks shuffling across the quilt's surface are another reflection of a playing card's two-sided nature.

Fallert originally was interested in pursuing a career in the arts, but the scarcity of well-known American women artists convinced her that the art world was not receptive to women. She chose instead to travel the world as an airline attendant, taking art classes in her free time and dabbling in stained glass and traditional quilting. During a layover in Buffalo in the early 1980s, she happened to attend a lecture by art quilter Jean Ray Laury and was inspired by Laury's successful career to set off in her own artistic direction with fiber. She soon was able to interpret the interaction of color and light—which had earlier attracted her to stained glass—through the fabric surfaces of her art quilts. Her work can be flat or three-dimensional and can be pieced, appliquéd, painted or embroidered; but color, light, line and movement are always strong elements. The spectacular skies that she sees while flying offer her a constant source of inspiration.

Fallert designed her Three of Diamonds on an IBM-style computer with CorelDRAW! software, which

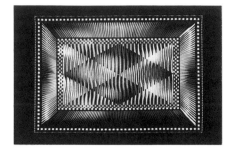

High Tech Tucks #31, 1991. 50 x 87 in. Hand dyeing, piecing, pleating and quilting.

allows her to visualize many pattern variations and to define the precise detail for which she is known. This high-tech approach to design matches the high-energy, space-age feeling of her quilts. Their futuristic quality has prompted their purchase for an impressive number of corporate collections, and they have earned a respected place for Fallert in the art world. However, on the backs of many of her quilts she includes a block done in a traditional quilting pattern as a tribute to all the quilters of the past who never were credited as artists.

THREE OF DIAMONDS

Hand dyeing, machine piecing and quilting, tucking. Cotton, cotton batting.

Gayle Fraas and Duncan W. Slade

EDGECOMB, MAINE

Born 1952, 1951

Yellow Moon, 1989. 33 x 25 in. Whole cloth quilt, dye painted on cotton. Photo by Dennis Griggs.

Gayle Fraas and **Duncan Slade** are two artists whose shared vision is the source of their collaboration both in their work and in their marriage. Since their first joint artistic effort in the early 1970s, when they were both art education students at Southern Connecticut State College, they have concentrated on the quilt format in their artwork. The two sometimes design quilts together as a team and sometimes singly. The painting on a particular quilt may be done by either one of them; they are equally skilled and prefer not to differentiate their work. Fraas does the final quilting and Slade sees to the mounting or framing of the piece. In the past they have each held various jobs in order to pay the bills, but since the mid 1980s they both have been full-time artists. By living modestly in rural Maine they can pursue their ideas "unencumbered by the market place."

Part of the vision that they share deals with humankind's stewardship of the land and one's response and responsibility to place. "Places are stories told through the remnants of history and the experience of their occupants." The landscapes that they paint address "the juncture where human involvement intersects the natural world." The artists sometimes use gameboards and playing cards as metaphors for games people play concerning land use and deals such as those made during the real estate boom of the 1980s. Fraas and Slade are saying, "How this land is used is not a game or just a deal; its use has long-term ramifications."

They choose to use the quilt format largely because of the enhanced emotional response elicited by the idea of a quilt and by textiles themselves. Often they paint borders around their landscapes that reference quilting traditions, or they juxtapose a textile design element against a wilderness scene. Their quilts have a very formal look, partly reflecting their interest in medieval manuscript illumination.

Fraas and Slade have experimented with many surface design techniques, such as batik, shibori, trapunto and others, but they prefer painting and screen printing with fiber reactive dye on a single piece of fabric. In this way they have maximum control over their visual imagery, without having the technique reveal the process. However, their methods remain flexible: "We're not material snobs; we're willing to explore anything." Thus on their Six of Spades they have set off the suitmarks with heat-laminated gold foil, and for recent architectural commissions they have painted aluminum panels with synthetic enamels.

With the Six of Spades, Fraas and Slade again allude to games and also to the "illusion of place." The unexpected arrangement of the panoramic coastline above the framed trees and sky hints that "a place is not always what it seems to be at first glance." The harlequinlike frames for the scenery—one painted in fanciful pastel shades and the other in deeper tones and stamped uniformly with Spade shapes for a richer, more formal framework—indicate differing perceptions of place.

Although the rocky coast scene and the pine trees on the Six of Spades represent specific locations, many of Fraas's and Slade's scenes are combinations of memories, idealized landscapes in the tradition of the Hudson River School of painters. The shadows that the artists sometimes place behind design elements also suggest the luminist emphasis on light. The illumination on this Six of Spades and its unspoiled wilderness appears to be coming from somewhere above, perhaps from a higher consciousness.

SIX OF SPADES

Whole cloth with dye painting, metal foil laminating, machine and hand stitching. Pima cotton, metal foil, metallic thread, polyester batting.

CAROL H. GERSEN

BOONSBORO, MARYLAND

Born 1947

Carol Gersen began her art career in the world of contract interior design, working as an intern while she was a student at Moore College of Art and Design. She continued to work in the interior design field for eight years after graduation, and in the last months of this period kept up a hectic commute between her company's New York office and her home in Philadelphia. The pace of her life changed abruptly, however, when she moved to a rural village in Maine and focused on the birth of her second child and the renovation of her family's house. In harmony with her new lifestyle, she took up quilting.

Gersen based her first quilt on an antique nine-patch block design that had been included in the 1972 Smithsonian show "American Pieced Quilts" and worked from a large bag of discontinued Merimekko fabric samples that a friend in the interior design business had given her. She then made several more quilts as copies of traditional patterns. In 1981 she studied with well-known quilter Nancy Halpern at Haystack Mountain School of Crafts and became totally immersed in her new art form. She started altering traditional patterns by skewing them or by adding or subtracting elements, and then she began inventing her own blocks.

Living in New England, Gersen was very aware of the contrast between the seasons and the sudden changes of weather, which were "a stunning part of life one could not ignore. The changes were so dramatic that sometimes they could be life-threatening if one was not prepared." In 1985 she began making a series of quilts exploring the seasons of the year. The next year, Gersen discovered dyeing. She began to dye fabric frequently, with various goals in mind: to obtain an extensive palette to choose from, to satisfy her curiosity and to obtain colors that had gone out of vogue and were not available commercially. She eventually turned to using her own hand-dyed fabrics exclusively in piecing her quilts because of the superior light fastness and unlimited color range she could achieve. In 1992, after over ten years of working in a very structured way, she suddenly found her meticulous process tedious and decided not to start with a pattern. She discovered that she really liked what happened when she worked loosely, not knowing what the end result would be.

Gersen's Ten of Diamonds is another quilt based on the seasons of the year, and she modeled her Diamond shapes on chestnut leaves in autumn. She dyed a variety of reds for the leaves and added in other hues to produce the spectacular colors that occur in the fall. She strip pieced the leaf triangles in the direction of the veins, pieced each whole leaf into a roughly rectangular background block and then assembled the blocks. Gersen

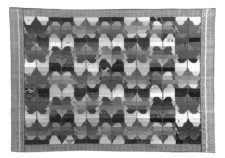

Leaves of Another Year, 1990. 59 x 84½ in. Cottons (many dyed by the artist with Procion dyes), hand quilting.

concedes that it would have been easier to appliqué leaves onto a background, but explains, "I am a piecer; I like the look of a smooth surface." She pieced by machine but did the final quilting by hand, incorporating both her signature and the date as well as many X motifs signifying the Roman numeral for ten. Quilted Xs are additionally positioned in the upper left and lower right corners to serve as subtle corner indices.

The ten Diamond-shaped leaves seem to fall randomly in Gersen's Ten of Diamonds quilt, but they approximate the actual arrangement of suit-marks on the card: a column of four Diamonds on each side and two in the middle. The shades of the leaves get increasingly deeper toward the bottom of the card, while the shades of blue that make up the angular sky background get lighter. Gersen's use of simple shapes and designs allows the subtle, skillful blending of colors and values in her intricate piecework to dominate her quilt.

TEN OF DIAMONDS
Machine piecing, hand quilting. Cotton (all fabrics hand dyed by the artist), cotton batting.

PATTY HAWKINS

LYONS, COLORADO

Born 1936

"I grew up in the South," says art quilter **Patty Hawkins**, "in the sterile fifties. We weren't encouraged to be creative." Nevertheless, she felt a continuing need to express herself in color and line and twenty years later decided to "work on this passion of being an artist." Vivid color and broad value contrasts have become hallmarks of her art quilts.

For a number of years Hawkins painted watercolors, but the translucent quality of that medium didn't provide the vibrancy she wanted. She began exploring quilting eight years ago and found herself creating the same kinds of images as she did in watercolor but on a larger scale and with the textural quality and strength of color possible in fabric. She finds much of her work inspired by the surrounding Colorado landscape, where "things seem bright and intense" and the sun is a pervasive influence. Not surprisingly, she finds herself infatuated with yellow. "I can't work without yellow; it's so vibrant. I love it though so many people hate it."

In her Six of Hearts, the playing-card symbols vibrate against a field of yellow, imparting a joyful feeling of vitality and optimism. The background of the card is constructed in a random, checkerboard strip-piecing technique, as are the appliquéd hearts, which creates a pointillist effect and adds depth to the color fields. The shadows produced by black fabric on the sixes

and a metallic gingham check on the hearts also give the illusion of dimension, and real dimension is added by swirls of beads that frost the surface. The curves of the Heart shapes are echoed in the curves of the sixes, in the patterns on the purple fabric from which the sixes are cut and in the sewing-machine "doodling" of the quilting. A jarring pink-and-black striped fabric forms the border and punctuates the piece. "I consider the predictable but usually do the unexpected."

Hawkins designed her quilt to be very clearly a playing card, but instead of including six Heart suitmarks, she has enlarged the corner indices so that they occupy the whole card. The resulting design has a playing card's double-headed quality, with the two sympathetically positioned Hearts suggesting the contrasts of the classic yin and yang interaction of opposing principles: positive and negative, bright and dark, masculine and feminine.

Indian Gap, Near Lyons II, 1992. 55 x 77 in. Cotton, cotton blends, metallic fabrics, beads, machine piecing and quilting.

SIX OF HEARTS

Random checkerboard strip piecing, machine embroidery and quilting. Cotton, cotton blends, lamé, rayon and metallic threads, beads, cotton batting.

diANe Herbort

ARLINGTON, VIRGINIA

Born 1951

Much of **Diane Herbort's** career in fiber art has focused on clothing design and embellishment. Armed with a bachelor of science in fashion design, she worked in the fashion industry for several years designing clothing for children, appliqués and other forms of embellishment and machine quilting. She eventually began working free-lance in response to her husband's frequent air force posting changes. Now she does graphic design work for magazines and pattern companies, regularly contributes embellished clothing and needlecraft projects to quilting and craft magazines and, with a partner, sells unusual embellishments and quilting supplies. She also coauthored two books of original designs with her sister, Susan Greenhut: *Old Glories: New Lives for Treasured Textiles* and *The Quiltwear Book*.

For the King of Hearts, Herbort designed an intricate confection of rich fabrics and elaborate embellishment that is a valentine of a playing card. The mirror-image symmetry of the composition plays intriguingly with the concept of opposites: positive and negative, youth and age, perhaps good and evil. Herbort strives for visual complexity in her work, and close scrutiny of her quilt reveals details unnoticed at first glance. For example, the central diagonal curve that unites the two kings is covered with a row of buttons, as if the two halves are buttoned together. Two subtly stitched

Hearts in the background encircle the kingly heads with their crowns of hearts. And finally, the quilt's binding is pieced to match each background color.

To begin her quilt, Herbort first drew the design full-size on artist's tracing paper and then perforated important design lines using a sewing machine. This garment-industry technique allowed her to accurately mark the fabric with white powder and provided a see-through pattern for quick positioning checks as the piece progressed. For the Kings' robes and the background, she created complex collages from tiny scraps of many different fabrics—men's ties, brocades, satins and velvets, among others—with random shapes that emphasize texture and play of light. Often she added more surface design with rubber stamps. On top of this fabric mix she placed embellishments such as buttons, sequins and lace and then covered it all with tulle, stitching everything together with free-motion machine embroidery and sewing around hard objects to hold them in place. She added programmed decorative stitches as accents and more embellishments on top of the tulle. "I love this stage but am always conscious of how easy it would be to overdo, so I try to question the need for each bead or charm." Herbort calls her technique "trash bag quilting," since although she searched for just the right fabrics for the King of

Hearts, the same technique could be used to salvage small scraps from the trash bag. She sees this method of quilt construction as an extension of crazy quilting.

In addition to her other free-lance endeavors, Herbort teaches her unique embellishment and quilting techniques around the country and has an ongoing role as a consultant to crafts cooperatives in North Carolina and West Virginia. In areas of little industry, gift items that are made through these cooperatives—mostly by women—and sold through shops in tourist centers often are an important source of a family's income. She meets with the cooperatives several times a year and advises on color trends and design improvements to create more cost-effective and marketable products, thus helping others to earn a better living through their skills.

KING OF HEARTS

Printing with rubber stamps; image transfer; machine appliqué, embroidery and quilting; hand embellishment.

Cotton, brocade, satin, velvet, lamé, lace, netting, beads, jewels, sequins, buttons, cotton/polyester batting.

dorothy HoLdeN

CHARLOTTESVILLE, VIRGINIA

Dorothy Holden loves color. She likes to play with it, to combine unexpected colors and see how they work together. Whether using subtle gradations of shades in a traditional pattern or a vivid and fearless palette in an original design, the emotional component of color is a strong part of her reason for quilting.

Holden's idea for the Five of Diamonds started with a checkerboard of hot pink and pale rose squares. She originally intended to add more shades of pink in Diamonds of different sizes, but when she happened across the strong, bright turquoise print the quilt suddenly came alive. She arranged her new turquoise Diamond suitmarks in a general circular pattern and was delighted to see a five-pointed star appear in their center, defined by their shapes. In a traditional quilt, a star motif would be constructed of diamond-shaped pieces also, but instead of a pieced shape, the star here is the result of the negative space created by the Diamonds.

Serendipity and happy accident are important factors in Holden's designs. The next compositional elements she added to her quilt were short strips of turquoise ribbons and finally a black passementerie cord. The cord tangled and coiled with a mind of its own, and when it independently began forming the number 5 in the bottom right corner, Holden kept the shape to serve as a corner index for the card.

The resulting Five of Diamonds is a playful, exuberant quilt that reflects its maker's intuitive approach to design. Holden constructed her checkerboard in a casual way and hand-quilted the squares in a similarly inexact fashion, reminiscent of a "naive" style of quilting. "I never do anything exact; I try to be inexact." The interplay of the floating ribbons, the willful black cord and the turquoise Diamonds suggests an image of wayward kites on a windy spring day. The youthful pinkness and the simplicity of the checkerboard background also bring to mind happy childhood pleasures of long ago.

Holden started quilting in the late 1970s when her husband's career signaled a move to Washington, D.C., and caused her to leave her own job as a school social worker. She began by making traditional quilts but always included her own innovations. As her work has evolved it has become less structured and more narrative, often with touches of humor, and she enjoys working with "found" materials. She refers to her free-spirited designs as unplanned and avoids intellectualizing about their creation. "I just do what I do when I'm inspired."

Day Star: The Winner. 60 x 60 in. The horse figure is composed of "singles" socks that have been appliquéd to an ikat background fabric. The horse's hooves are sequined.

FIVE OF DIAMONDS

Machine piecing, hand and machine appliqué, hand couching and quilting. Cotton, sateen, passementerie, polyester batting.

Melissa Holzinger

ARLINGTON, WASHINGTON

Born 1951

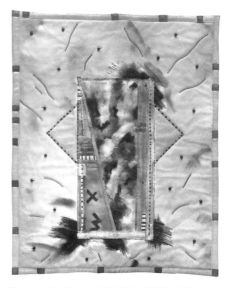

Beyond the Pale, 1994. 36 x 29½ in. Mixed media, fabric assemblage, machine quilting.

Melissa Holzinger first took up quilting in 1982, after being "electrified" by the work of well-known quilt artists Nancy Crow and Michael James. She had been introduced to fabric assemblage and silk dyeing in 1975 when she was in art school, so she again used silk and hand-dyed all her fabric for her first quilt. She taught herself quilting techniques from books and religiously did all stitching by hand. Her first quilt took her six months to complete, but she had discovered her medium.

From the very first Holzinger designed her own patterns, exploring the effects of color, movement, depth of field and pattern. But unvaryingly, she planned her quilts according to a grid and used geometric shapes. Her work always had easily identifiable connections to traditional quilt making. She worked in a very controlled way, making gouache maquettes beforehand and leaving nothing to chance. She meticulously cut templates for her original block designs, and when she wanted to work with curved seams, she cut paper shapes to use as interfacings for each small piece, in the English tradition.

The year 1993 became one of transition for Holzinger. It began with an invitation from Nancy Crow to do five new works for a show by April. Holzinger felt honored to be asked and made the five quilts, but the pressure of the deadline intensified her growing dissatisfaction with her tedious working methods. More and more, she was angered by the rigid set of quilt-making rules and steps she imposed on herself and decided that she needed a more spontaneous and innovative way to use her quilt-making knowledge and experience. She experimented with the faster and more direct method of painting her fabric with acrylics instead of dyeing it, and she switched almost totally to sewing by machine so that she could keep up with the ideas that raced ahead of her hand-sewn stitches.

A thematic shift accompanied the technical shift in Holzinger's work, and she moved from studies in design to more personal expressions concerning intellectual and emotional issues. Her Eight of Diamonds is very much a part of her transitional period. In reflecting on playing cards, she could recall only negative feelings. She remembered the "eternity of boredom" when she had been forced to play canasta as a child or to play endless games of gin rummy with her first husband. (After that she had avoided men who played cards.) She therefore channeled her negative emotions into her Eight of Diamonds quilt, choosing heavy canvas instead of finer broadcloth and sewing with embroidery floss and metallic cord to make stitches that look like sutures.

She made no preliminary drawings for the Eight of Diamonds. For the red of the Diamond suitmarks (the color of blood and anger), she painted the canvas with acrylics that she rubbed roughly around to blend as many shades as possible. She then drew in the wet paint with pastels, enjoying the sensation of grinding the crushed pigment into the red paint. Afterward she cut her painted canvas into random strips blindly, by working from the reverse side. For the background spaces she painted other canvas to suggest cold, rigid, metallic surfaces. The resulting quilt is a "crazy log cabin," and though it has roots in a traditional pattern, it looks nothing like her earlier work. And, though it is tied like a comforter, it is not comforting.

With her new spontaneity in design, Holzinger is forcing herself to trust her instinct and her experience, saying to herself, "I know what I'm doing!" She recognizes that the anger she felt at her highly controlled quilting methods also reflected frustration at constraints on herself as a woman that didn't make sense anymore. Her new coarser materials represent a toughening-up process. "If I'm going to have a niche in this world it's not going to be one traditionally awarded to women; I'm going to have to carve it out for myself. I have to be the one to give my work meaning." Carving her own niche is not just opting out of motherhood and other roles expected of women. It's also opting into art, legitimizing herself in a field not known for its recognition of women.

EIGHT OF DIAMONDS

Canvas collage, painting, drawing, airbrush, machine stitching, hand embroidery and tying.
Cotton duck, nylon and metallic thread, cotton batting.

SANDRA HUMBERSON

BALTIMORE, MARYLAND
....
Born 1947

The Ace of Hearts has been **Sandra Humberson's** card for a long time. Together with other icons that have come her way, that card has been pinned to her studio wall ever since she found it lying face-up on the city sidewalk outside her door in 1989. As she proceeded to work on her Ace of Hearts quilt, she came to feel that this was truly the card she has been dealt, and which she has chosen, throughout her life.

Humberson began her Ace of Hearts by screenprinting the continuously written word "memory" on many pieces of hand-dyed fabric. She then cut the fabric into strips and reassembled it into diagonally strip-pieced lengths that she arranged in a chevron pattern for the background. She cut the heart shape from the drop cloth she had used in the printing process, which contains the elusive shadows of "memory" as well as some "memories" that are carefully appliquéd to its surface. Numerous rips and tears in the heart are in various stages of being sewn up by real needles threaded with red silk. Narrow ribbons of fabric that she cut from old clothing are scattered over the background and echo the shape of the steel needles. Humberson machine stitched an aluminum border around the heart and around the quilt itself.

Opposites have a strong attraction for Humberson: micro and macro, order and chaos, metal and cloth. The chevron background pattern is a combination of opposites, as is the nature of the needle: "It pricks and sticks, mends and makes the most lovely and delicate stitches." The contrast of fabric and metal fascinates Humberson because she also sees their similarities. They both "can be transformed in so many ways. Both become richer with patinas of scratches or faded and fraying threads. These are the layers of history that invite our memory, imagination and emotion."

Memory and emotion are often themes of Humberson's work, and the heart is their province. Her Ace of Hearts is a metaphorical piece with many layers of meaning. The needles may be mending a torn heart, sewing up memories, or reworking them, restitching them into new forms. A needle is a constant companion to Humberson; she "would be lost without one." She sees it as a symbol that "connects generations of women, our histories, our loves and depressions— and our emotions to our lives. The needle is the instrument that has given us voice."

Fabric has been Humberson's medium all her life. She studied painting and other formal disciplines while working on both her B.F.A. and M.F.A., but professionally quilting has been her medium of choice. She has taught printmaking and nearly always prints the fabrics she uses in her quilts. She sees the progress of her

Collected bits and pieces on Humberson's studio wall. Most were found around the same time as the Ace of Hearts card.

artwork not as linear but circular, "constantly picking up tangents" from where she's been. She was putting metal on quilts twenty years ago, for example, but in pieces such as the Ace of Hearts she is reworking her vision, combining these contrasting materials with the added perspective and emotions of the intervening years.

ACE OF HEARTS

Screen printing, machine piecing, hand and machine stitching, trapunto, embellishment. Hand-dyed and printed silk, cotton and linen blend fabrics; aluminum; steel needles; cotton and silk thread and embroidery floss; polyester batting.

HoLLey Junker

SACRAMENTO, CALIFORNIA

Born 1936

"You Can Run But You Can't Hide" is the title of **Holley Junker**'s Jack of Hearts. This Jack is the tricky Knave of Hearts who stole the tarts in *Alice in Wonderland*, and now he is running away with them and trying to hide. He almost succeeds in disappearing into the background camouflage, perhaps into the colorful crowds of a tinselly town.

Junker's recent quilting style has involved overlapping a multitude of small fabric patches to optically blend colors in a pointillist manner. She usually combines solid and patterned fabrics in closely related shades to create color depth, but she took the opportunity of interpreting the Jack of Hearts to "play a little," using vibrant patches of Mylar to create a psychedelic field of pulsating color which almost swallows Jack. "The trick of it was not getting him completely lost."

Junker created the pointillist background by cutting out small circles with a pair of pinking shears, setting them in place on a muslin backing with a dab from a gluestick and securing the whole surface with machine quilting in a small grid. She copied Jack's face and general shape from an antique English playing card made around 1800 and added other details suggested by *Alice in Wonderland* drawings. She embroidered parts of his costume and foreground, producing a textural surface that contrasts with the shiny background and keeps

the figure from completely disappearing. The large red Hearts and Jack's banner are cotton appliqués, and his staff, which forms the letter J, is made from metallic corded thread. Jack is proffering a bouquet of Heart-shaped antique Venetian glass beads in his outstretched hand, and smaller glass beads are trailing from his staff and floating away into the Mylar.

As is the case with so many quilt artists, Junker came to the medium in a roundabout way. She has thought of herself as an artist for most of her life, and on graduation from high school she won a scholarship to a prestigious art school. However, her family would not let her accept it, choosing instead to send her to secretarial school so that she would always be able to support herself. She did as she was told and took art courses when she could. In 1974 she was able to enter school full-time and earned a B.F.A. from the University of New York two years later. By this time she was skilled in printmaking and drawing but avoided painting, mainly because she found mixing pigments in proper proportions a difficult chore. She began to develop an interest in what could be done with needle and thread.

In 1978, while working as a volunteer at a museum bookstore, Junker became intrigued when a customer urgently sought a book by someone named Jean Ray Laury who made quilts. When a lecture and

Bluegreen Dreamworld, 1991. 34 x 34 in. Pointillist technique of pinked fabric patches that overlap and are machine stitched in place. Photo by Sharon Risedorph.

workshop series by Laury was advertised, Junker signed up for one of each out of curiosity and "discovered the art quilt revolution." Up to that time she had felt a bit like an artist without a medium, but suddenly the idea of using textiles to create art was a perfect fit, and her artistic life was changed.

The Queen of Hearts, she made some tarts,
All on a summer day;
The Knave of Hearts, he stole those tarts,
And took them quite away!

JACK OF HEARTS
"You Can Run But You Can't Hide." Machine appliqué, hand and machine embroidery, embellishment.
Cotton, Mylar, velvet, metallic threads, perle cotton, antique beads, paint, cotton/polyester batting.

Natasha Kempers-Cullen

BOWDOINHAM, MAINE

....

Born 1949

Somewhere, Somehow, 1991. 38½ x 25½ in. Painted, embellished quilt. Photo by Dennis Griggs.

Natasha Kempers-Cullen is an artist who believes that we can create our own reality. Her reality is a world in which we "walk in partnership in order to assist in the healing of the earth." Her art quilts are windows through which an ideal world shines with beauty and clarity, a hopeful place in which each tiny part is important.

Her Seven of Spades is a "Green Quilt," a loving tribute to Mother Earth. Kempers-Cullen chose this card primarily because the suitmark's resemblance to a garden spade would give her a context for creating a fertile garden scene of peace, health and abundance. She also liked the number Seven because of the symbolism that it often carries. In the garden, the seventh month of the year, July, brings warmth and sunshine and is a prime growing time. The seventh day of the week is a day of rest, and so her seven spades are idle, in their proper places in the toolshed temple that is the focal point of this idyllic landscape. This garden shrine is at the center of a rainbow of meadows and fields, with birds and bees overhead and a stream running close by that is alive with fishes and frogs.

Kempers-Cullen painted this pastoral scene with fiber reactive dyes on a solid piece of cotton fabric, although the distinct areas of color and pattern give the quilt a pieced and appliquéd appearance. Embellishing is just as important as painting to Kempers-Cullen, so she searched for buttons, charms and appliqués of growing things—cows, sheep, bumblebees, strawberries, tomatoes, etc.—to make her painted quilt come alive. She sees the two techniques together creating a unified whole and can't imagine using one without the other. The embellishment process for the Seven of Spades was "pure, non-stop fun," which she was sorry to see finally come to an end. Once she had decided to embellish the piece heavily, however, she realized that she would need some very special spades. So she drew the shape she wanted and asked a metal-worker friend to cut seven brass spades for her, and then she blackened their blades with spray paint. For an additional Spade motif, she cut a small stamp from a rubber eraser and used it to stamp Spade-shaped leaves on the tall trees and the canopy of branches that frame the picture.

Kempers-Cullen learned to sew and do many fiber techniques from her mother and two grandmothers and went on to major in studio art in college. For sixteen years she taught art full-time in various Maine and Massachusetts public schools. Since 1987 she has been teaching at national quilt conferences and at Haystack Mountain School of Crafts, and she serves in schools as an artist-in-residence, sharing her vision and techniques with students. One of her most rewarding recent experiences has been her work at Spindleworks, an artists' and weavers' cooperative for the developmentally disabled.

In her own artwork, Kempers-Cullen saw a definite direction develop only after she began combining painting and fabric. In her early quilts she focused on technique, but now in her art quilts she focuses on ideas. Most recently the idea that she has wanted to express has been concern for the environment and its care. She wants to challenge, excite and inspire by creating upbeat quilts that contain "a healing flow of energy" and a message of hope. Instead of getting up on a soapbox and being angry all the time, Kempers-Cullen chooses to make statements that are positive, and to do so quietly through her quilting.

SEVEN OF SPADES

"In the Garden." Whole cloth with hand painting, stamp printing, machine and hand quilting, beading, hand embroidery, embellishment. Cotton, textile ink, dye, buttons, beads, charms, custom-made brass spades, metallic threads.

katHerine Knauer

NEW YORK, NEW YORK

Born 1952

Katherine Knauer made her first quilt in 1976, spurred on by the impulses of the American bicentennial and a new baby. Five years and twenty traditional quilts later, she grew restless and started to think about making quilts that would "say" something, although at the time she wasn't sure what she would have to say. As it turned out, her addiction to watching television news soon gave her endless subject matter.

Her quilts began to reflect things she was thinking about, and "conflict" became the general theme of much of her work, the "generic universal combat" of men against each other, against women or against technology. She also saw it as a metaphor for her own psychological tensions. Her husband's interest in military history helped to educate her in the mechanics of war and gave her a visual vocabulary for reflecting on the inevitability of conflict and the pervasiveness of war in our society. The family's collection of reference books on uniforms and weapons provided her with imagery that she has used repeatedly.

Knauer continues to admire the patterns and symmetry of traditional quilts and uses them as the basis for most of her pieces. The irony of interpreting violent, disquieting themes in a medium known for order and comfort adds to the dark humor of her work, and with her fondness for puns and sense of the absurd, her war quilts

are decidedly humorous and satirical. She chose the Four of Clubs for its symmetrical possibilities and the ominous symbolism of the suit. In her resulting symmetrical card, the four club-wielding cavemen almost seem to be enjoying their battle ritual, stepping in time to some primitive martial music, doing do-si-dos around a four-hand star of their war clubs.

Knauer's introduction to the airbrush and heat-set fabric paint in 1984 led to experimentation with stencils and a new direction for her work. She had wanted to do figurative imagery and discovered that stencils are ideal for creating repetitions of the same shape. She combined the quilting tradition of repeated images with her inventory of war machinery and was soon producing borders of grenades and airplanes. She began printing most of the fabric she used in her pieces, making possible twill patterns of machine guns and falling bombs. For the Four of Clubs, Knauer used stencils to create the marauding cavemen, the background color blocks and the clubs, all on a solid piece of cloth. She sometimes applied the paint by hand and sometimes by airbrush for added translucence. The "drips and spatters" of the overall background are limited to the colors of the blocks, as are the polka dots in the border. It is fundamentally a simple piece, in keeping with its primitive subjects. To retain the absolute symmetry of

Tabloid Baby Quilt, 1992. 50 x 50 in.

the card, she signed it twice, in opposite corners.

Knauer's color palette for her war quilts tends to be grayed. She avoids pure colors, particularly blue. "Blue is the most beautiful color and tends to make everything around it beautiful." For studying war, she uses everything but blue.

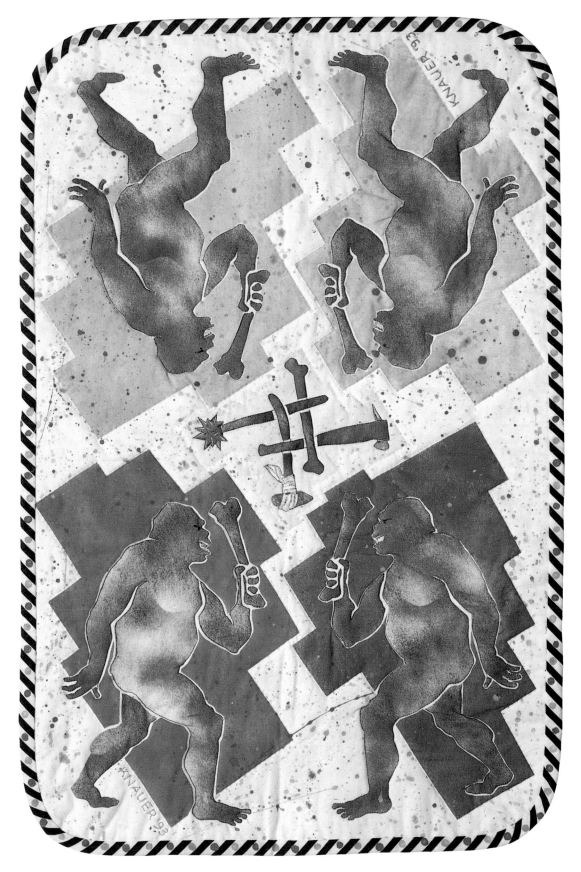

FOUR OF CLUBS

Whole cloth with hand stenciling, airbrushing, hand and machine quilting. Cotton, polyester batting.

jeAN rAy LAury

Born 1928

Jean Ray Laury is a name well known to many quilters. She teaches quilting both in this country and abroad, is the author of at least ten books on quilting and folk art and has been inducted into the Quilters Hall of Fame. She has a firm historical sense of the role of quilts and their development, but in her teaching she stresses that contemporary quilts need to reflect their makers.

Laury makes it clear that she has great respect for traditional quilts. In her own work she often employs their conventions, such as symmetry and repeated blocks, and frequently includes familiar quilting motifs. But she depicts them in lighthearted ways, and her quilts delight the viewer with her intelligent sense of humor. Her message is that there is no need to slavishly copy traditional designs. Creative people should not deny themselves "the opportunity that quilt making affords for self-expression" and should feel free to personalize quilts and make them relevant to our times. The world is changing, women are changing, and traditions are often being stood on their heads. "Traditional designs no longer meet our needs."

The Eight of Spades was the card that Laury was assigned, but it did not meet her needs. She had been hoping for a queen so that she could once again incorporate the image of her own smiling face, a picture of herself

that she has finally learned to be comfortable with and like. After many years of hating the way she looked, she tried to get over it by having rubber stamps made from pictures of herself and then stamping her face over three yards of fabric. She proceeded to use her face in various contexts as a repeated image ("Multiples are compelling; it's particularly hard to ignore anything that is repetitious") and in illustrious company (George Washington and Abraham Lincoln, among others). Now, she says, "I still get a kick out of sticking my own photo into various spots." Her solution to the mundane Eight of Spades was to include her personal Queenly design as a medallion in the center of a traditional number-card format.

Laury also took liberties with the definition of a quilt. The project guidelines called for three layers of fabric, but instead of the usual front, batting and backing, she used three layers of felt. Felt is one of her favorite materials because of its beautiful, intense colors and because its matted texture permits a cut edge to act as a finished edge. It allows "small forms and complex shapes or letters that would otherwise be almost impossible to appliqué if the edges had to be turned." Simple running stitches hold down the edges of the felt.

Laury is attracted to the whimsy in everyday objects, and so on her Eight of Spades she holds the tools of her

Barefoot and Pregnant: The Senator Van Dalsem Quilt, 1988. 44 x 44 in. Photo by E. Z. Smith.

trade in her hands instead of a face-card Queen's scepter and flower. The electric iron and the strip of slides refer to her recent enthusiasm for photographic transfer processes, most of which require heat. (For this piece she used her Thermo-Fax, "a somewhat ancient" imaging machine but a purchase which she considers one of her wiser investments.) The result is a very proper and conservative-looking card—until one examines it more closely. Queen Jean, ruling with her ruler, flirts with the viewers and invites them to share the joke. It is the ultimate in self-expression!

EIGHT OF SPADES

"Jean of Spades." Photo emulsion silkscreen; hand painting, appliqué and quilting. Cotton, felt, cotton/polyester batting.

Mickey Lawler

Mickey Lawler's Two of Diamonds presents two shimmering red stars in a night sky, casting down their reflections on an illusory surface below. The shattered darkness of the starry night and the gossamer quality of the ground owe much of their ethereal effect to the hand-painted fabrics with which they are constructed. These "Skydyes" are Lawler's own creations and have become the focus of her artistic career.

Lawler first started dyeing and painting fabric in the early 1980s, when she had begun using unusual fabrics in her quilts and felt frustrated by the limited selection available commercially. She started tie-dyeing when a firm making tie-dyed fabric discontinued the line, but she soon switched to fabric painting because of the greater variety of effects she could achieve. Her first painted fabrics were for use in her own work, but in 1985 she inaugurated her business, Skydyes, and began selling her fabric to other quilters.

She now spends up to twelve hours a day painting cotton, working in her home workshop on four sixteen-foot tables. In order to produce interesting textural patterns, she experiments with using unusual materials as tools, such as feather dusters and ice crystals, in addition to the more ordinary brushes and sponges. She tries to create abstract and natural effects of rocks, gardens, water and, of course, sky. She uses a variety of textile paints and inks, favoring those that give the translucent effect of watercolor.

Lawler created the fabrics that make up most of her Two of Diamonds by using a combination of sponges, brushes, squeeze bottles and sprays and by spattering paint from a brush. She chose a variety of red satins and silks for the two stars and added the red lines of reflection with strips of adhesive red metallic paper. She diagonally pieced the sky in the direction of the stars' reflection and machine quilted rings that radiate from a ghostly moon. The striking contrast of geometric precision and the celestial setting creates the impression of two brilliant red satellites orbiting in space.

Lawler's first career was as an English teacher. She took up quilting in 1969 when she spent much of her time at home with her young children. She studied the quilts her grandmother had made and read a few books on the subject before starting out on her own and later gained some art training through workshops and symposiums. She describes her first quilts as "very traditional and boring;" as a beginner she didn't dare even to mix prints. (She felt very brave the first time she used paisley!) Since then, she has written articles for quilting magazines, coauthored the book *Not Just Another Quilt*, taught quilting and fabric painting extensively and painted thousands of yards of Skydyes.

TWO OF DIAMONDS

Hand painting, machine piecing and quilting. Silk, cotton, blends, brocade, Mylar, taffeta, lamé, metallic thread, cotton/polyester batting.

Libby Lehman

HOUSTON, TEXAS

Born 1947

One might say that **Libby Lehman** received her early quilting education from her mother, but not in the usual sense. When Lehman was pregnant with her first child, her mother signed up both her daughter and herself for a beginning quilting class. At the time, neither realized that quilting would eventually become a new career for each of them. Since 1979, Lehman has been exhibiting her quilts and teaching workshops around the country. Her mother, Catherine Anthony, went on to open a quilt shop of her own in Houston during the 1980s and to teach classes and show her quilts nationally. Mother and daughter joined forces to coauthor four quilting books on block patterns and grids.

When her mother brought well-known teachers to her quilting shop, Lehman signed up for their classes. With the inspiration of teachers such as Michael James and Nancy Crow, her traditional style of quilting gave way to art quilting. The innovative sewing machine techniques taught by Janet Page Kessler also proved to be an important influence on Lehman, who became an active adherent of the machine-quilting movement of the late 1980s. She became intrigued with using thread as part of the design statement instead of just for quilting stitches to hold layers together. She began to use a variety of metallic and rayon threads in her work and developed an original machine embroidery technique that gives the effect of translucent ribbons dancing across the surface.

Lehman's Ace of Clubs shows a precious gem blazing with fire, set against a vibrant patchwork background of rich jewel-tone fabrics. She constructed the Club through reverse appliqué and embellished it with metallic threads that add excitement and brilliance. She used a free-motion machine-embroidery technique both on the Club and for the background quilting and used her distinctive sheer stitching for the corner indices, giving a translucent, shimmery effect to the superimposed images. For these she chose a lower-case "a" instead of the usual uppercase letter in order to echo the curves of the Club suitmark. To outline the teardrop shapes within the Club and for the inside border of the quilt, Lehman employed "bobbin drawing," a technique by which she is able to sew with decorative thread that is too large to go through the eye of a needle by winding it onto a bobbin and sewing blindly from the reverse side.

Lehman specifically chose to interpret the Ace of Clubs in honor of a favorite card game of her local poker club. One game that the group sometimes plays is "High and Low Chicago" in which a player automatically wins if he or she draws the Ace of Spades. The members of the group found themselves feeling sorry, however, for the suit of Clubs because it is the

Hidden Agendas (detail), 1994. Lehman uses her sewing machine to create "thread-painted" areas and to draw with lines of satin stitching.

lowliest card suit and a Club is never a winner. So the poker club made up a game and named it after a Texas town, calling it "High and Low Nacogdoches." The Ace of Clubs is the winning card in this game.

ACE OF CLUBS

Machine embroidery, reverse appliqué and quilting. Cotton, rayon and metallic thread, cotton batting.

LiNdA LeViN

WAYLAND, MASSACHUSETTS

Born 1937

Linda Levin is intrigued by the interplay of forms that creates the illusion of transparency, the balance of complex patterns and strong, clear structural elements. Her art quilts have deep, mysterious shadows that suggest other realities in the midst of the solid, tangible present. "I think a lot about the real and the imaginary, the imaginary being much more interesting."

Levin's quilts are done in a painterly manner and usually are restricted to a narrow range of color and value. In order to get the brushed color effect that she desires, she uses many methods to apply dye to her own fabric, sometimes creating many yards at once without a specific project in mind. She would like her work to "approach painting while retaining the tactile qualities of fiber art." She keeps her pieces relatively flat by using cotton flannel in place of a quilt's traditional batting. Her collagelike technique—in which she builds the quilt top directly onto a fabric backing—and the raw edges that she leaves exposed "give a spontaneous, direct, painterly feeling." The translucent shifting and fracturing effects that she achieves have a decided cubist flavor and strongly reflect the influence of painter Lyonel Feininger. "I care a lot about his work and connect with it on an absolutely visceral level." Recently she also has been developing an interest in the bold, intense colors and abstract compositions of Stuart Davis.

The formal aspects of art have interested Levin for a long time. She earned a B.F.A. in college but wasn't inspired by her academic education to become a studio artist. Instead she detoured to marry and raise a family. She always sewed, however, and began dyeing fabrics first for craft projects and then for quilts. She credits quilt artist Nancy Halpern with "liberating" her and encouraging her to trust her own artistic sensibilities. She has been a full-time fiber artist since 1980 and currently has a studio in her home.

Levin bases many of her quilts on scenes from her travels, portraying landscapes or cityscapes with fragmented and repeated architectural elements. The human figure on the face card she chose therefore presented her with a unique challenge, which she met by constructing an abstract Jack of Spades with her characteristic translucent geometric shapes. She "simplified the options by working with the givens." Her card actually follows its original model very closely. She limited her palette to the traditional face card colors of red, black and yellow, although with an unusual emphasis on the yellow. "I don't use red. I'm interested in contrast, and yellow and black are the strongest contrast. In this piece the other colors have to work with

Invisible Cities III, 1990. 42 x 71 in.

the yellow instead of the other way around." Her Jack is seen in one-eyed profile, but in place of a halberd he holds a Spade in his hand like a goblet. His courtly curls turn up in a flip and conveniently form a J to serve as a corner index; another J is formed by his handlebar mustache. Levin sees this Jack as a knave, a trickster twirling his mustache. "Old movie villains always had mustaches; heroes never did."

JACK OF SPADES

Hand dyeing, machine piecing and quilting. Cotton, flannel batting.

M. JOAN LINTAULT

CARBONDALE, ILLINOIS

Born 1938

Joan Lintault's realm is the natural world. Her quilts for the last few years have all been "Green Quilts," celebrating the interconnection of every living thing and the earth's "self-regulating, self-maintaining system." She has always felt free to explore and use any technique that contributes to her work and doesn't reject a method simply because it is laborious. She bases her work "on geological time rather than TV time."

The Ten of Clubs was Lintault's immediate card choice. When she was a small child first starting to play cards, the Club was the only suitmark she could identify as a real thing—a clover leaf in the grass—and so in order to have as many clover leaves as possible for this quilt, she asked for the Ten. Her ten clover leaves are hiding in a grass jungle that is inhabited by snails, snakes, turtles and insects. Clover flowers and other plant life join the grass-blade network that supports this miniature crawling world. Lintault individually silkscreened each of the designs on cotton fabric that she had hand dyed in the greens, browns, purples and oranges of the natural world, and then she added more details and color with a paint brush. She cut out the shapes and stuffed them, connecting the pieces with a sewing-machine lace technique that makes the images appear suspended in space. In her Ten of Clubs quilt, Lintault has exactly reproduced the layout of the original card in the

arrangement of the suitmarks, the number ten in each corner and the design's double-headed symmetry.

Lintault studied art education in college and went on to earn an M.F.A. with a focus on ceramics. When she had difficulty getting access to a kiln she began working in fiber and has been teaching in the fiber department at Southern Illinois University for over twenty years. She became a quilt maker after seeing some old quilts at an auction in the mid 1960s, prompting her to say to herself, "I can do that!" Her designs have never been traditional, however; she immediately began creating original figurative images, qualifying her as one of the earliest art quilters.

Lintault had enjoyed using natural dyes to produce natural colors in the wool yarns she used for weaving, and she attempted to get the same effects on cotton fabric for her quilts by using fiber-reactive dyes, with their added colorfastness. The study of natural dyes and dyeing methods was one of the things that took her to Japan in 1984–1985, under a Fulbright-Hays Research Fellowship. As a student of Japanese art she responded to a sense of mystery in it, a spark that "seemed to fit." Being in Japan, however, turned out to have a profound influence on how she felt about nature. Lintault distinctly remembers watching a friend paint flowers for eight hours, wondering at his intensity. Trees,

Mountain Torrent (detail). Sewing machine lace suspends the hand-printed fabric leaves of this dimensional quilt. Photo by Frances Loyd.

flowers and animals had always been important to her, but after this she began to look at things differently. "Nature is scary, mysterious, something we can't" control. Why does the Mississippi flood? Why is this insect crawling across my kitchen floor? Why does anything happen?"

TEN OF CLUBS

Hand dyeing; screen printing; painting; stuffing; machine piecing, embroidery and quilting. Cotton, beads, string, polyester batting.

LINDA r. MacDONALD

Linda MacDonald's recent quilts suggest illusions of underlying realities, universes that may be "revealed and made finite yet remain untamed." She deals in fields of space "moving in counterpoint" to other fields of grids, lines and small objects. Her designs are minimalistic yet contain allusions to the materials of building and also to the interlacing of fiber. She enjoys using the randomness of chance occurrences to generate patterns and images. Since it was chance that she drew the Seven of Clubs (it was the only card left), she used its shapes in her card quilt as random design elements, without attention to symbolism or inherent meaning.

Her Seven of Clubs is a maze of tiny overlapping patterns of neutrals on neutrals that she has painted onto whole cloth. She began by dyeing the background an uneven gray, depending on wrinkles in the cloth and a casual approach to the dyeing process to produce random coloring. She then airbrushed areas with black paint, using various objects either as stencils or resists to create light and dark shapes. Small sticks, pieces of toys, refrigerator racks and the grids of nursery seedling trays all contributed to her patterns. Using a small brush, she highlighted details and emphasized spatial relationships with black and white paint. As a final touch, she

created another field of space and illusion with the stitches of free-form machine quilting.

MacDonald's involvement with quilts began in 1974, when she and her artist husband were living in the country in remote Northern California. She had studied painting and various textile arts but had never considered quilting as a modern art medium until she got involved in the quilting project of her weekly women's "rap group." She was very familiar with family quilts from Ohio, but to her they had seemed dated and locked in the past. Now, however, she began to see possibilities in this indigenous American art form with its illusionistic images.

In 1974 she was unaware that anyone else was making contemporary quilts, and her efforts were experimental as she began to break up the traditional repeated-block format. She came to appreciate the ease with which she could create images in quilting, compared to her earlier weaving, and the "largeness of the image window" of a quilt. By 1980 she had switched to quilting entirely. Since then, her geometric landscapes with illusions of dimension and subtle pastel color gradations have given way to more monochromatic planes and layers of space. MacDonald feels rewarded by the "fusion of disparate elements," the contrast of her cool

Amphora (detail), 1990. Dyed, discharged, airbrushed, painted and stitched.

geometrics on the soft, warm quilt fabric. She is convinced that the American quilt is "the arena of a new frontier."

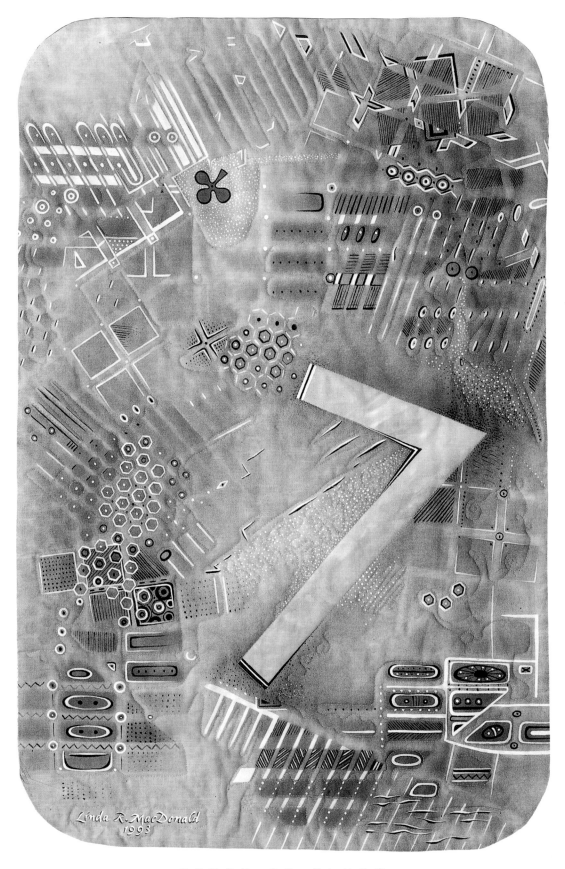

SEVEN OF CLUBS

Whole cloth with hand dyeing and painting, airbrushing, machine quilting. Cotton, acrylic paint, cotton batting.

Marguerite Malwitz

BROOKFIELD, CONNECTICUT

Born 1947

The art quilts of **Marguerite Malwitz** reflect her love of travel and good scenery and capture the images in her memory as stylized fabric snapshots. She was daunted, however, by the challenge of fitting her trademark landscapes into a Two of Hearts motif until she recalled a recent vacation in Bermuda where her family loved discovering two separate, enchanting worlds. On land they delighted in the island paradise of pink sand, lush foliage and wonderful architecture, and snorkeling adventures opened up the hidden undersea world of corals and fantastical fishes.

Her Two of Hearts is based on a photograph of "the coral pink house across Grotto Bay," a favorite sight because "the color of the house is a reflection of the colors of the beach." In the top half of the piece the shape of an inverted Heart envelops the colorful buildings. A matching Heart, a sea fan waving in the gentle currents, is reflected in the blue water below but is almost invisible. "As in snorkeling, one's eyes must adjust before seeing the undersea scenery."

Malwitz often uses appliqué for the structure of her quilts, and for this piece she tried a collage variation, sewing fabric pieces directly onto washed artist's canvas. It is a very spontaneous way of working and one that she enjoys immensely. The Two of Hearts incorporates screen-printed fabrics from the British Virgin Islands,

commercial and hand-painted fabrics and her own cyanotype images. She used rubber stamps to create some of the passing fish in the water scene and the rows of palm trees on land. Other embellishments include metallic threads accenting the flowing currents, buttons forming coconuts in the palm tree and a real shell lying on the beach. In the water she suggests a bed of seaweed by the addition of various long narrow fabric strips, reminiscent of other Bermuda quilts she has made. Over the land she scattered Matisse-like floating leaves.

Malwitz studied arts education in college and found her niche in crafts. A stimulating semester working as an apprentice in the weaving studio of instructor Ina Golub led to a twenty-year working association between the two. She not only executed the pictorial tapestries that Golub had designed but also shared in technical troubleshooting and in many other operational decisions in the studio. Along the way, she received an excellent education in color and design and learned the business side of the art world. In the late 1980s Malwitz switched from weaving to quilting and adopted her mentor's "big story-picture" approach for her quilted landscapes. Now she works in her own studio attached to her home on a heavily wooded lot, where the landscape outside is on constant view through her many windows.

The Creation, 1994. 61 x 59 in. Photo by Brad Stanton.

TWO OF HEARTS

"Bermuda Hide and Seek." Blueprinting; rubber stamping; spray painting with resist; paint washes; machine appliqué, stitching and quilting. Cotton, linen, silk, buttons, beads, shell, metallic thread, polyester batting.

there/e
MAY

Therese May's quilts began their giddy life in the dream world of her childhood. While both sleeping and daydreaming, May used to be visited by a fantastic collection of real and imaginary creatures that she has never forgotten. Once she started to make quilts, she realized that this was a way to bring back to life these childhood friends, and she has been doing so with happy abandon ever since.

Although May studied formally to be a painter and received a master's degree in fine arts, her approach to quilting has been entirely intuitive. In 1965 she leapt into this traditional craft in her own way, inventing her own methods and breaking rules she didn't even know existed. Struggling for a time between conflicting desires to paint and to quilt, she finally realized she could do both and started painting on her quilts.

Her designs begin with a general layout plan and hand-drawn images that she cuts out and uses as templates for appliqués. Once she gets started she adds other details as they seem appropriate. Sometimes she creates designs and then decides what they are. She embellishes freely with beads and buttons and dabs of paint, and she leaves connecting sewing threads uncut to create a network of texture over the surface of the quilt.

For the Queen of Clubs, May decided on a playing card's traditional double-headed format because it would give her "the chance to draw two people with funny animal hats on." The Queens share the same heart in the center, "only the center has a Club in it because that was my card." Being Irish, May saw the club as a shamrock, and the figures became Irish female leprechauns. "All in all the Queen of Clubs is quite a magical card." Instead of a scepter next to the Queen there is a snake, another symbol of power. The card's border is a pieced braided rug pattern, a nod to a traditional quilting technique and a symbol she frequently includes as a reference to hearth and home. The blue-and-black background suggests the nighttime world of dreams, and scattered everywhere are the shapes of eyes and stars.

May's fantasy creatures are never threatening; rather, they are good-humored playmates. They often stick out their tongues at the world to proclaim their independence and the importance of "making fun," and this is the sort of message May is sending with her playful quilts: art is one of the few places where people can let go and say and do anything they want. Her name is a statement of her artistic philosophy: "Therese may." She gives herself permission to do whatever she whimsically and artistically wants.

Twins (detail), 1992. Shown are some of May's embellishment with beads, buttons and high relief dots of paint.

QUEEN OF CLUBS
Painting, machine appliqué, embellishment. Cotton, polyester, buttons, beads, gems, safety pins, polyester batting.

CAROLYN L. MAZLOOMI

CINCINNATI, OHIO

Born 1948

Carolyn Mazloomi came to art quilting neither by tradition nor by training. No one in her family sewed, and her education was in aeronautics rather than in art. As a child she had always been fascinated with airplanes and went on to get her pilot's license as well as a Ph.D. in aerospace engineering. By chance she saw her first quilt in the late 1970s and heard it saying, "Come to me!" She began buying books and proceeded to teach herself to quilt.

Mazloomi's current quilts are often narratives that express the endurance, suffering and courage of her African-American ancestors or which explore today's challenges. "Analyzing our past helps us to understand the present and gives us strength to continue to exist." She wants to communicate clearly, favoring simply drawn pictures and appliquéd images, and she frequently incorporates materials from her extensive collection of African fabrics.

Mazloomi decided to make the Nine of Spades an obvious playing card but also to celebrate African-American culture through its design. She created the Spade suitmarks with pieces of a cotton print from Sierra Leone that acquired its sheen from a polishing with cassava starch. The black background fabric is also from Africa, a commercial batik that she has hand quilted with images of West African ceremonial masks. She embellished the quilt with cowrie shells brought back from Ghana by a friend. In earlier days cowrie shells were used throughout Africa and the Pacific as money and could therefore be fitting embellishments for playing cards, which cause money to change hands when cards are used in gambling.

Mazloomi has been instrumental in bringing attention to African-American quilts and is writing a book on the subject, to be called *In the Spirit of Cloth.* In 1983 she founded the African-American Quilt Guild of Los Angeles. Whenever she traveled in the United States or abroad, she always looked for quilt shows but rarely saw the work of black quilters represented. She came to realize the isolation of many minority quilters and their need "to get in touch" with each other, so she founded another organization, the Women of Color Quilters Network. What started as a network of seven members in 1985 grew to 750 by 1993, with ten chapters in the United States and many others throughout the world. The membership encompasses minorities from many cultures, united by the fact that the influences on their quilting come from other than European traditions.

When Mazloomi first began making quilts, her work was very traditional. She read about historical quilts and couldn't imagine anything more splendid than a Baltimore Album quilt. As time went on, however, she found herself growing disenchanted with

The Family. 66 x 42 in. Hand painting, piecing, appliqué and quilting. Cotton.

these models that seemed more and more foreign to her. Finally, on one memorable day in the late 1980s, she burned all of her Baltimore Album quilting books in the fireplace. "It was a release of the spirit!" Ever since then she has been doing "what feels good," not worrying about color combinations, just following her own instincts. She feels as if deep down she always knew what she wanted to do. "It was always there."

NINE OF SPADES

Hand appliqué and quilting, embellishment. Cotton, shells, metallic thread, polyester batting.

katHerine Mckearn

TOWSON, MARYLAND

Born 1954

Katherine McKearn's artistic training has been in music. She played the French horn and studied orchestral performance at the Manhattan School of Music in New York City, where she lived for eight years and worked as a free-lance musician. Now a suburban housewife and mother, she has turned her artistic expression toward quilts. She sees parallels, however, between musical performance and art quilting. "You must be technically sure of yourself to make things appear spontaneous. As a colleague used to say, you must play with 'controlled abandon.' A quilt is the same; it must look spontaneous but all the little stitches take time to make."

McKearn feels that a quilt should reflect its maker, and so her quilts usually end up being quite complicated because "a lot goes into a person." Her work is currently taking two different directions: album quilts and mask quilts. Her album quilts personalize the traditional album format by incorporating scenes and symbols from her present life. Her mask quilts follow the repeated block tradition, but each block is an independent mask. She was drawn to masks because they symbolize the ability to "try on" faces, to display emotions without having to really feel them. By putting on the mask of an angry housewife, for example, one can show the necessary emotions elicited by a particular situation without commit-

ting to a permanent role as a shrew. Her Eight of Hearts is done as part of her mask series. The eight Heart suitmarks are actual masks with sad, tortured faces and eyeholes that a small face could look through.

In much of her work, McKearn enjoys emphasizing underlying chaos. She says she used to be a perfectionist in everything she did, on the theory that if she did things perfectly, everything else would be perfect, too. But now that she has discarded that delusion, she revels in leaving frayed edges in her quilts, stitching strips on slightly askew and mixing fabrics that don't match at all. Instead of relegating the quilting stitches to an unobtrusive overall background pattern, she spotlights them by using bright colors, textural stitches such as French knots and substantial threads. She likes to quilt with perle cotton because of its sheen and because its strength allows her to draw the fabric up as she goes, producing a richly textured surface. The resulting multidirectional pleats of her quilts echo "the never ending tug-of-war" of her own "domestic chaos" produced by trying to juggle the conflicting needs of her artwork, husband and three children.

McKearn's Eight of Hearts includes her characteristic frayed edges, but only within borders. All outside and inside edges of the quilt and its masks are neatly bound, as if containing the chaos. The technical skill and ingenuity

of her work belie the fact that she has been making quilts only since 1990. For this quilt she chose fabric with colors that reminded her of the colors on face cards, and her card quilt has traditional playing card symmetry that makes it equally readable either right side up or upside down. As she was working on the Eight of Hearts, McKearn remembered her grandmother playing daily games of solitaire, which perhaps was her own way of dealing with the domestic chaos of her family of eight children!

EIGHT OF HEARTS

Fabric manipulation, hand stitching. Cottons, metallic fabrics, cotton batting.

barbara Mortenson

Born 1942

Barbara Mortenson is an art quilter known for cutting right to the core of an issue. When faced with the task of representing a Heart, she considered creating a frilly, sugary valentine but couldn't force her scissors to cut one out. A Heart is a heart. Her Ten of Hearts, therefore, shows ten life-size, anatomically correct life pumps.

Mortenson searched extensively for the perfect heart image, finally finding it in an old children's book about hearts that she came across through her job as a children's librarian. By using dye paper she was able to change the black-and-white Xeroxed image to magenta. "This is not an ailing heart; it is beating strongly." The irregular shape seemed to need the strength of uniform repetition, so she chose the traditional suitmark format of ten full-frontal views.

In her work she likes to use bold colors, so as a contrast to the magenta hearts she painted mostly shades of green and yellow onto layers of canvas, chintz and sheer nylon and polyester. In between the layers, or through them all, she machine embroidered using bright yellow, green and red threads. Using a rubbing technique, she transferred textural pattern from a piece of hat netting to the top layer of sheer, to echo the zigzag of her stitching. The combined result gives the effect of translucent tissues of the body through which a network of buried veins and nerves are half-visible. The hearts, which are fused onto a top layer of sheer fabric, take on a sculptured appearance from many intricate lines of machine stitching. Mortenson explains that although her quilts don't deal with "pretty concepts," she likes to make them beautiful pieces of art. "Depending on what your situation is, a healthy heart can be a beautiful sight."

Mortenson's quilting experience had been limited and fairly tame until she happened to see a quilt exhibit in 1980 that opened her eyes to the medium's possibilities. Her reaction was immediate: "I always wanted to be an artist. I sew. I can do this!" She started by personalizing traditional patterns and then in the mid 1980s began making art quilts in earnest and has kept on growing. She loves the idea of breaking loose from restrictions, because with luck, wonderful things are released.

When Mortenson first agreed to make a card she was at an emotional low point, so she wanted to choose the luckiest, most auspicious card there was. Her research told her that in fortune telling, a Heart was a sign of good fortune and happiness, and the Ten of Hearts was good luck ten times over. "What's better luck than ten good hearts?"

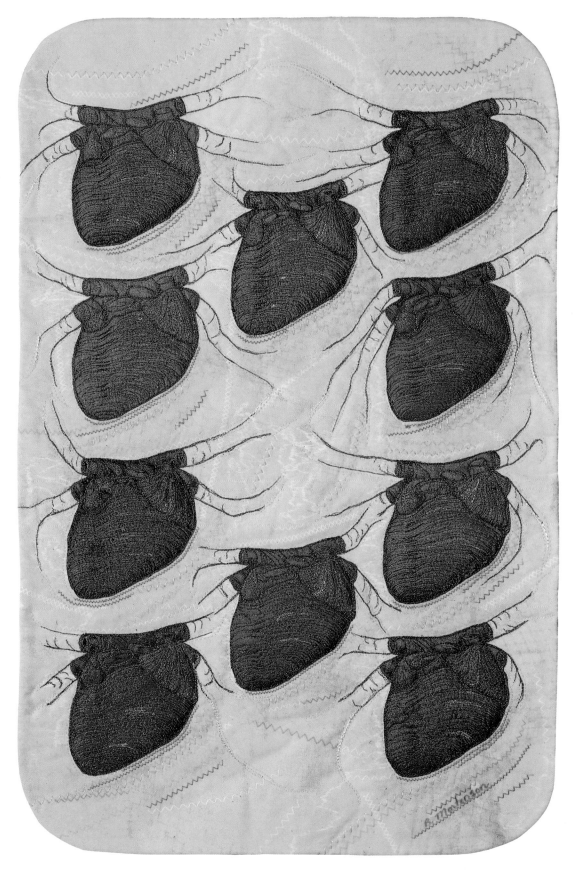

T E N   O F   H E A R T S

Fusing; rubbing; dye transfer; painting; machine appliqué, embroidery and quilting. Cotton, organza, polyester, netting, polished cotton, rayon and metallic threads, polyester batting.

dominie NASH

BETHESDA, MARYLAND

Born 1939

One of **Dominie Nash's** greatest rewards as an artist is in the creation of fabrics to use in her quilts. She has always loved playing with color and seeing what she could do with it, whether dyeing yarns in ikat patterns for weaving or controlling color areas with wax resists in batik. For her quilts, she has experimented with a number of printing methods for adding overall patterns and impressions of texture to her painted cottons, rayons and silks, which she combines in abstract assemblages. Many of her printed fabrics have tie-ins to gardening, a favorite activity, and she often roams about using her camera as a sketchbook, capturing interesting textural images in vines, plants or the paving stones on an old terrace.

Nash's Five of Spades, with its recognizable garden spades, is a departure from her usually abstract work. The riot of fabrics, however, is typical and clearly displays her printing virtuosity. Some of the fabrics are "monoprints," produced by pressing the cloth against a surface of ink into which a texture has been impressed. Others are "photoscreens" in which she has transferred an enlarged photographic detail to a silkscreen. Sometimes she silkscreens repeatedly on one piece, creating layers of design as well as of color.

Nash works in a collage manner, designing and adding more layers as she goes. For the Five of Spades, she started with a black-and-white printed background and added a layer of different black-and-white prints in the shape of pentagons, as an allusion to the traditional "Grandmother's Flower Garden" piecework pattern. Her design decision was influenced by the discovery that the five-sided shapes, which she had chosen as a reference to her playing card's number, do not fit together the way the usual hexagons do. She thus chose to space the pentagons evenly like repeated blocks against another background fabric, introducing a subtle complexity of patterns. She cut the shapes for the colorful flowers from fabric that she had printed with stencils created from the images of real flowers. The resulting similarity of all the prints gives a transparent effect to the flower appliqués floating on the surface, even though the fabrics are opaque.

When she was growing up, Nash never thought of studying art. In school she found that her art classes emphasized good drawing skills and so they were a struggle for her because she "didn't draw." Instead she took degrees in social work, going as far as completing course work for a Ph.D. but never really enjoying the subject. In the 1960s she fortunately learned to weave—an art form that did not require drawing skills—and also to do batik. She soon embraced these as outlets for her creative expression. She studied many weaving techniques

Peculiar Poetry 3, 1994. 43$^{1}/_{2}$ x 42$^{1}/_{2}$ in.

but most enjoyed experimenting with methods of dyeing yarn in order to control color placement. At the time there were very few books on dyeing and it was difficult to find anyone with experience, so she often learned by doing. She went on to write a monograph on warp painting, making use of her knowledge of weaving and application of dyes.

In 1985 she moved into a studio whose physical space made it possible for her to work on a large scale for the first time, and she began making quilts from her cast-off batiks. Today, her quilts are made entirely from her hand-printed fabrics and reflect not only the patterns from her garden but also the colors of Bonnard and the lyrical abstractions of Diebenkorn, "with their wonderful light."

FIVE OF SPADES

Screen printing, machine appliqué and quilting. Cotton, textile paint, polyester batting.

kathLeeN o'coNNoy

The Joker is the enigma of the card deck. It has no place of its own yet has the power to upset the hierarchy of the other cards and to interrupt a rational game of skill in an all-powerful and capricious way. It represents sanctioned cheating, the transformation of the meaningless into the meaningful and vice versa.

Kathleen O'Connor's Joker was influenced by the Jungian "shadow" figure, a combination of the fool of medieval church carnivals and the Tarot and of the Native American trickster. Her Joker is both male and female, both the wise man and the clown; part human, part animal and part divine. It is a mongrel creature that shows at least three faces to the world: a hook-nosed conniver gazing out to the left, a simpleton in the center and a third figure in profile on the right. This Joker carries a skunk-like doll on a stick in order to talk to itself and holds a keyboard in reference to the fool's traditional association with music. The word "zero" is spelled out in the top right corner and refers to the card's lack of a numerical value. The many circles on the piece are other references to zero and also to this character's full-circle completeness.

The Joker was a natural card choice for O'Connor, whose collagelike quilts are combinations of disparate elements. She enjoys putting together materials that are odd or awkward and watching what happens when they meet and clash. Her design process sometimes begins with a sketch, but soon a piece takes on a life of its own and, as she puts it, she just "tags along." She usually works with her own hand-dyed or painted fabrics because of both the control and the surprise they provide, and she uses the technique of appliqué because of its spontaneity. She works quickly and directly, welcoming the results of this process that produces both failures and discoveries.

This quilt is on a much smaller scale than O'Connor's usual very large, often oddly shaped pieces, and it is also unusual because it is made mostly of commercial fabrics. However, it is very typical of her assertive, abstract designs that evoke the essence of their subjects. O'Connor's characteristic bold colors, ambiguous shapes and frond-like details combine effectively to produce a clownish, deceitful Joker.

O'Connor began her formal artistic education in her last semester of college, when she took a few art courses and realized that this was what she "should have been doing all along." She went on to earn a B.F.A. in painting several years later, studying with artists Jacob Lawrence and Michael Spafford, but gave up that medium when she became pregnant and worried about the turpentine fumes associated with oils. Instead

The Ace of Cups, 1993. 8 x 8 ft. Research on cards for the Full Deck led O'Connor to the Tarot deck in which the Ace of Cups symbolizes creativity and renewal. It seemed a particularly worthy subject.

she made baby quilts and then other quilts that soon began looking like paintings.

In both her painting and her quilting, O'Connor has been strongly influenced by the cubism of Picasso and Braque and, as they had been also, by the model of African sculptures. Her portrayal of the Joker, who can have different identities at different times, appropriately illustrates the cubist interest in the relativity of time by presenting the figure as sage, fool and animal all at once.

JOKER

Machine piecing, appliqué, embroidery and quilting. Cotton (some hand dyed), cotton batting.

LiNdA S. perry

LEXINGTON, MASSACHUSETTS

Born 1951

Linda Perry's artistic concerns are the expressive use of color and imagery and the nuance of light. Her distinctive quilts are rich constructions of fine fabrics and fine craftsmanship that present a sensual, lush appearance.

Her Seven of Hearts is a good example of Perry's recent quilting style. The quilt's architectural motifs make reference to her long-standing interest in art deco design, and the precision of the composition reflects her mathematical training. Her quilts are sometimes "artistic vignettes" that interpret tales from Greek mythology ("I always love a good story"), and she often includes astrological prints among her fabrics. She has signed the Seven of Hearts in this quilt's central sphere as if she were a constellation.

Perry sometimes hand dyes her fabrics, as she did for the blue backgrounds on this quilt, but she also uses a wide range of commercial and antique cottons and silks. The extravagant floral prints in the side panels are Japanese textiles that she has bordered with fabric strips painted a metallic gold. She embellished the seven Heart suitmarks in the upper right corner by pressing gold-colored metallic leaf against randomly spread adhesive within a Heart-shaped stencil. The commercial jungle print used as a background near the top of the card includes a toucan who conveniently has assumed the shape of a 7 and serves as the playing card's corner index.

As a young girl, Perry very much wanted to be an artist but was advised against it as an impractical career. Instead she trained as a mathematician at the University of California at Berkeley. Her interest in art was rekindled, however, by an interim job as a scientific illustrator at the Berkeley Botanical Gardens. After graduation she proceeded to take art courses and worked as an illustrator in the physiology and botany departments of her alma mater. When her marriage took her to Boston, she worked for a while as a math teacher and as a software engineer, but she also studied design and color theory at Harvard and drawing and painting at the School of The Museum of Fine Arts. A local quilt show in 1982, and particularly the work of Ruth McDowell, opened her eyes to the artistic possibilities of the quilting medium. She enrolled in a very traditional quilting course because she wanted a firm grounding in techniques, but she soon took off in her own direction. "I quilt like I cook; I can't abide to follow a recipe."

Leda. 47$\frac{1}{2}$ x 38 in.

S E V E N   O F   H E A R T S
Hand appliqué, machine piecing and quilting. Cottons, metal leaf, polyester batting.

sue pierce

ROCKVILLE, MARYLAND

....

Born 1944

Sue Pierce discovered the joy of collecting and putting together interesting fabrics when she made a "crazy quilt" intended as a wedding gift for her brother in 1975. A career as a professional quilt artist was not what she had envisioned as a math major in college, but after her first foray into quilting she went on buying fabric and experimenting. In 1985 Pierce took the decisive step of renting studio space at an artists' cooperative so she could pursue her artwork full-time. Since then, the style of her work has ranged over such varied formats as repeated pictorial blocks, geometric abstractions and even spontaneous fantasy creatures inspired by the color and imagery found in the folk art of many cultures. She finds that she learns from each style and relates its lessons back to the others.

Recently Pierce has been working on a series of quilts that explore the subject of German doors in a quasi-realistic pictorial style. The series had its roots in a seven-week stay in Germany in the fall of 1989, when Pierce accompanied her husband on a business trip. She was left to her own resources most of the time, and because she spoke little German, she found herself focusing more sharply on what she was seeing. She roamed through towns with her camera, collecting images that she might later use in her artwork. Frequently she was drawn to the architecture of humble

structures that had survived centuries of time, buildings whose doorways and windows had witnessed the passage of ordinary people for as many as six or seven hundred years.

Pierce's Nine of Diamonds is part of her "German Door" series. Her building materials for the structures in this picture were commercially printed fabrics. "I like the idea of working with materials that already have some information attached to them." However, she distressed the walls with a translucent "stain" of thinned acrylic paint to give an aged, worn look and added machine-quilting to suggest the texture of peeling plaster. With a thick machine-embroidered satin stitch, often in a contrasting color, she drew in details and outlined pictorial elements. She favors this technique because it covers the raw edges of appliquéd shapes and at the same time creates a cartoonlike effect. The picture's basic composition and architectural details were suggested by one of her photographs, but she has added characteristic small, humorous touches, such as "breaking" one of the window panes to show the requisite number of Diamond suitmarks. Pierce's scene has a warm and friendly Old World look, and the viewer expects the door at 9D to be opened in greeting any minute.

Pierce is a strong believer in the value of networking and mutual support among artists, particularly in an emerging art form such as art

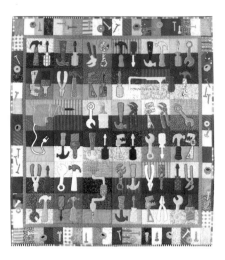

Tools of the Trade, 1992. 57 x 50 in. Machine appliqué. Photo by Breger and Associates.

quilting. Nationally, she is on the board of directors of the Studio Art Quilt Associates, and locally she has become known as an arts "enabler," helping to launch several arts organizations and exhibitions in the Washington, D.C., area. Says Pierce, "I get a great deal of satisfaction out of making connections, recognizing need and talent and putting them together to help make things happen." However, she considers herself primarily an artist and is happiest when she is in her studio designing quilts.

NINE OF DIAMONDS

Machine appliqué, embroidery and quilting; staining with acrylic paints. Cotton, blends, polyester batting.

YVONNE PORCELLA

MODESTO, CALIFORNIA

Born 1936

Yvonne Porcella first made a name for herself as a designer of clothing, not of quilts. She is the author of six books—on color, projects for painted fabrics and designs for pieced clothing based on ethnic patterns. She is a person of high energy who teaches herself what she needs to know as her interests have led her from one activity to another.

Porcella's degree was in nursing, not in art, and for nineteen years her workplace was a hospital operating room. Her interest in clothing developed over many years of sewing clothes for herself and her four children, and in the process she educated herself in the principles of clothing construction and tailoring. A desire for unique fabrics led her to weaving, which in turn led her to studying ethnic clothing for its flat construction methods and minimal tailoring. She soon found that the modular construction of many ethnic garments invited combining a variety of fabrics, and thus her quilted wearable art pieces were born. When one of her pieced and quilted kimonos was accepted into the prestigious Quilt National show in 1981, she moved on to creating actual quilts.

As Porcella moved away from the functional and into the world of art, she began teaching herself art theory and art history in order to give her work direction. She also began teaching quilting extensively and showing her work both nationally and internationally. Out of a perceived need to promote recognition and respect for the burgeoning Art Quilt medium, in 1989 she organized Studio Art Quilt Associates, the first serious national organization for quilt artists, and continues to serve as its president.

Porcella's Five of Hearts is a good example of her own current quilting style, which tends to be bright and graphic with narrative content that is set into a strong geometric framework. Her subjects and her quilts are usually good-humored and cheerful and have playful themes that recall happy times. They are viewer-friendly, frequently including polka dots, stars and game board patterns as well as familiar American cultural images.

The red-and-black checkerboard in her Five of Hearts is machine pieced and has a border suggesting green felt; the black-and-white tile floor of the background is also pieced. Over the piecework, Porcella hand appliquéd the food and the Hearts that are floating off the board and hand painted the bottle of Five of Hearts beer (her invention). She hand quilted the piece by outlining the various shapes and by stitching the number 5 into the upper left corner.

Porcella-the-Artist's concept in this interpretation of the Five of Hearts is the association of card playing with the frequently parallel activities of eating and drinking. In addition,

Pet Paradise, 1993. 44 x 60 in. Photo by Sharon Risedorph.

Porcella-the-Former-Nurse sees a heart as an important part of a healthy body and wants to remind the viewers that card playing is a sedentary activity and the food that accompanies it is often junk food. She hopes that people will remember to be good to their hearts.

FIVE OF HEARTS

"The Poker Party." Machine piecing; hand appliqué, painting and quilting. Cotton, polyester batting.

eMiLY
richardson

Emily Richardson has spent much of her artistic career as a costumer. She has interpreted characters through their clothing for repertory theater, Philadelphia's two opera companies and the Pennsylvania Ballet. When she found herself contemplating the character of the Jack of Clubs she was perplexed by his inscrutability. Who is Jack? A knave or a prince? A bad seed or an Irish lover? Is he a boy or a man? Of all the Jacks in her deck of cards, he was the only one without a mustache. Is Jack a female playing a "pants role"? To Richardson, he seemed to be part male and part female. She decided to emphasize the mysteriousness of this character, an impostor who performs different roles while keeping his (or her) true nature concealed.

To create this Jack of Clubs, Richardson limited herself to four colors in keeping with the Aristotelian theory that the nature of all things is determined by the arrangement of four basic elements. She selected silk and linen fabrics that offered the obscuring properties of veils, scrims and sheers and painted them in the colors of red (fire), yellow (air), green (water) and violet (earth). She began to cut out shapes by following the contours of the paint, and through this process an illusive, androgynous form appeared, taking shape from the materials of concealment. She cut a variation of the form to create a

general mirror image and her composition was under way. Throughout the process of composing and refining her design she saw Diamond, Heart and Spade shapes appearing, as if the Jack of Clubs were made up of parts of all four suits. To confirm the identity of the card as a Jack, Richardson included in each corner a subtle letter J in all of its reversed and inverted manifestations.

The final Jack, says Richardson, "exists in four quadrants. The right and left sides reflect each other nearly literally in terms of shapes, though there is variation in the colors. The bottom is meant to reflect the top, but more like two sides of the same coin, or as though the top is the image we see and the bottom is the image that we don't see; that is, the other, possibly darker or more mysterious side of a person, or the person's self-perception. In any case, it reflects the complexity of character. Who is the Jack? Certainly neither male nor female, but a character consisting of four images, making one ambiguous picture." The transparency of the layered materials allows for a play of light and shadow, alternately revealing and obscuring at different layers of the composition. To the viewer, Richardson's Jack of Clubs suggests a Rorschach test in which the identity of the image is subject to one's associations.

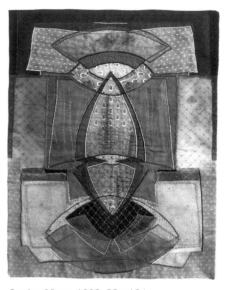

Garden Muse, 1992. 22 x 18 in.
Photo by Rick Fine.

Richardson began making costumes in college and went on to earn a bachelor of science degree in fashion design and to build a career as a free-lance costumer. In the mid 1980s she began making quilts, partly in response to the Amish quilts "with their stunning colors" and partly due to the combined influences of a slack time in her work and the availability of wonderful scraps. A workshop with quilter Nancy Crow in 1988 opened her eyes to quilting's potential as an art medium. Her familiarity with the theater tends to make her see things as "staged," and her experience with manipulating fabric and working with a variety of textiles gives her ample tools for mounting her own personal art quilt productions.

JACK OF CLUBS

Hand painting, appliqué, embroidery and quilting. Raw silk, raw linen, cotton, cotton/polyester batting.

deidre scherer

The subject of playing cards as an art study interested **Deidre Scherer** long before the Full Deck project came about. In 1980 she began making a series of fabric and thread pieces based on the double-headed Queen images from playing cards. Wanting faces with more depth and character instead of the cartoonlike figures usually depicted on cards, she studied pictures of various people, including Native Americans, but eventually decided that she needed to draw real people using live models. Her search for "wise, Queenly figures" led her to nursing homes, where she began spending many hours doing drawings and listening to the stories and memories of her models.

Scherer's studies in the nursing home profoundly influenced the direction of her future art. She became fixated on the richness and experience reflected in faces that are shaped by ninety years of living and feeling. She abandoned her playing card project to concentrate on trying to bring out the essence of her elderly subjects' lives and at the same time to communicate the impact that their faces were having on her. For one thing, she found a model for aging, and for the first time she was able to imagine herself growing old.

Scherer chose to work in the medium of fabric and thread collage, responding to materials that had expressive textures and patterns of their own. Her fabric portraits have a very painterly appearance, however, reflecting her original training as a painter while working on her B.F.A. at the Rhode Island School of Design. As her work has become known, she has been honored for her sensitive depiction of the elderly by having her fabric portraits selected for use on posters and as cover art of publications connected with geriatrics as well as with art.

Her technique is to draw with her scissors, cutting basic outline shapes for the background and then sculpting the images by adding additional layers of shapes to suggest planes and shadows. She pins the layers together and then draws some more with the sewing machine, using a zigzag stitch not only to hold the pieces in place and to secure raw edges, but also to shade and create subtle transitions between adjoining colors and textures. She often oversews several times, choosing thread color carefully and changing stitch length constantly.

The Full Deck brings Scherer's work full circle. She chose the King of Spades to interpret and used a photograph of her father as the model for the King. "Initially the King of Spades had the myth of heavy power; now I'm feeling more benevolence behind this figure." This may explain the soft blues and browns of the

Harmony, 1993. 11 x 10 in. Photo by Jeff Baird.

fabrics she selected instead of the red and gold traditionally used for face cards. Once she began to work on the project she found that progress was surprisingly slow, and she says she sometimes felt emotionally blocked. "Is this the power of cards and their symbolism? Is it combining the image of my father with the image of the King of Spades?"

KING OF SPADES

Cutting and layering; machine appliqué, embroidery and quilting. Silk and cotton fabrics and threads.

JOAN SCHULZE

SUNNYVALE, CALIFORNIA

....

Born 1936

When **Joan Schulze** was asked to interpret a playing card, she knew immediately what kind she would make. Her mother had died the year before, and among her things Schulze found many decks of cards that her mother had been unwilling to throw away after they were worn out. "I had been mulling over what to do with them. As I flipped through the decks, I noticed that many of the pips were worn away, had cracked or just had ghostly remnants of their original shape." Schulze knew that she wanted her Three of Spades to be a reflection of these old cards that she remembered her mother using to entertain visiting grandchildren and, so many years ago, Schulze herself as a child.

The design came together quickly. "I eliminated making it too far away from normal card faces. I remember how much my mother disliked playing solitaire with some 'art cards' that I had given her many years ago." Schulze had a previously pieced cloth on hand that she decided to use for the background for the card. She printed the Spade suitmarks on it using the kind of transfer liquid used for printing T-shirts. In order to get the worn, faded look of the old cards that were her models, she cut Spade shapes for the transfer images out of greatly enlarged black-and-white photographs of Florida, where her mother had lived.

Schulze usually works in an abstract style, but she includes elements in her representational Three of Spades that are common to many of her quilts. "I use lots of diagonals, do things in asymmetrical ways; I put an exciting color or rich texture off to the side. This means that I have somehow made that composition work, or that area would appear to fall off the piece." Since her work is so subtle, she frequently uses black to draw people's attention. "It marks the areas where I want them to come close. I've watched, and it works." Schulze tries for "a little anxiety" in her work, something that almost makes it not work. "I don't want it to be safe." If a quilt doesn't excite her, she cuts it up and recycles it into other pieces.

Schulze is also a poet and is published regularly in the poetry quarterly *Orphic Lute*. She frequently writes poems inspired by individual quilts or, conversely, makes quilts inspired by her poetry. During the designing process, she often stops to make notes or write down combinations of words that have occurred to her. Sometimes the poem will be finished before the quilt, and it will tell her what the quilt still needs. Her poems, like her quilts, are impressions of the moment, pages in a journal. "Life has always been my subject, a running commentary on day-to-day events." She considers that the

Return to Eden, 1992. 47 x 47 in. Photo by Sharon Risedorph.

complexities of life are appropriately expressed in fabric, "which endures so many magical changes . . . a perfect metaphor for life."

THREE OF SPADES
Photo transfer, painting, dyeing, hand and machine stitching. Cotton, silk, paper, cotton batting.

robiN SCHWALb

BROOKLYN, NEW YORK

Born 1952

In the Aztec culture, the gods were believed to be mortal. If not properly nourished with "precious water" (human blood) and "red cactus fruit" (human hearts) they would die, and all life on Earth would perish. **Robin Schwalb** has chosen this gruesome mythology for the basis of her compelling Three of Hearts. Her "purposely naive" style, imitating manuscripts contemporary to the sixteenth century conquest of Mexico, and her meticulous craftsmanship combine in a quilt that powerfully contradicts the usual saccharin image of a heart, which "suffers every indignity of clichéd and sentimental representation."

Schwalb chose the details of her design from a variety of Aztec arts. She based the double-altared temple on the Great Temple of Texcoco and drew the sun character from an image of the sun god Tonatiuh that appears on Aztec calendars. She copied the human figures from various manuscripts and positioned them appropriately, with two victims having just made the ultimate sacrifice and a third falling down the steep steps, his heart a projectile flying toward the eager and hungry sun god. Europeans have added explanatory text to the drawings in most native manuscripts from the period, so in the upper right corner Schwalb has written an explanation of the Aztec practice of human sacrifice.

The subject matter of the Three of Hearts is very unlike Schwalb's previous work, but it includes some common elements: the written word, a wry sense of humor, architectural motifs and a sense of action. "I like to have a flow across the surface of the quilt"—blood, in this case. She cut stencils for many of the images and then either stenciled on fabric, cut out the images and appliquéd them to the background or else stenciled directly onto the quilt's surface, "a nerve-racking process" that left no room for error. She outlined the human figures in black in order to draw attention to them and used light charcoal gray for all other lines. She hand quilted the background with small cross-stitches; outline quilted the temple, figures and sun and contour quilted the hearts to reflect the pulsing of their still-beating state.

Schwalb's art training was in painting. After college she studied a number of craft and art techniques and took a job as a hand weaver for Dan River, Inc. By chance she became a skilled projectionist, and for the past twelve years has worked in that capacity at the Metropolitan Museum of Art. Her profession has some influence on the perspective she uses in her quilts, which frequently include scenes frozen as if on film. Her deep interest in communication in general and in the beauty and meaning of language is a strong element in all her work; no quilt of hers would be complete without some form of the written word.

Babel, 1990. 72 x 90 in. Photo silkscreening, stenciling, painting, machine piecing, hand appliqué and quilting. Photo by Bob Malik Studios.

Schwalb was moved to interpret the Three of Hearts in the way she did by a crisis in her marriage. She and her husband separated in early January 1993, "a terrible, terrible time" during which she felt like her heart was literally being ripped from her body. Happily, they were reunited shortly before Valentine's Day, but the quilt remains as a memento of that time, lest they forget at their peril what led to their separation and how they worked things out.

The mortal gods felt hunger and thirst. They were nourished with precious water and red cactus fruit. Thus through death was life sustained.

THREE OF HEARTS
Stenciling, hand appliqué, machine piecing, hand quilting. Cotton, polyester batting.

KATHLEEN SHARP

MONTE SERENO, CALIFORNIA

Born 1945

Kathleen Sharp is a master of spatial illusion, an artist who builds expansive marble-walled structures within the confines of her two-dimensional quilts. Her architectural images evoke feelings of airy, timeless space, creating a metaphysical bridge between fantasy and reality. Using the soft medium of fabric, she creates rooms within rooms that appear to be made of solid stone.

The cool, marble rooms of Sharp's Nine of Hearts become warm and appealing as the Heart suitmarks float in through the windows and doors to come home to the viewer. Each of her Hearts represents a heart "condition," and she has embroidered their names on the back of the quilt. From front to back the hearts are Stout, Light, Wise, Full, Burning, Broken, Faint, Sad and Dear. Sharp also observes that in card games "it is often advantageous to have many cards from one suit," so she has given her piece the title "Calling All Hearts" and machine embroidered it on the wall trim above the door.

When Sharp was first invited to interpret a playing card, she decided to trust fate for her choice and pulled her card at random from a full deck. The role of destiny in choosing her card was confirmed for her several weeks later when she coincidentally came across a Nine of Hearts lying by itself in the sand on the beach. For her Nine of Hearts quilt, she used the traditional flat techniques of piecework and appliqué and did all stitching

by machine. She occasionally paints or dyes her fabrics, but for this piece she used all commercially printed cottons and cotton/rayons. The fabrics she selected and her careful attention to perspective make the squares of marble flooring look real, and the pattern of the wall fabric and her quilting lines give the effect of building blocks. The sense of dimension and movement that she creates seems so real that the viewer is tempted to step out of the path of the advancing Hearts.

Sharp's interest in architecture has been lifelong. When she was twelve or thirteen she wanted to become an architect but ended up pursuing a career in mental health instead and directing her creative energy to painting and to taking art courses. She had been interested for some time in making quilts, so while living in Washington, D.C., she studied traditional quilting with area resident Elly Sienkiewicz, the quilter and historian who brought attention to Baltimore Album Quilts. Sharp's desire "to do art" found its home in quilting, and in 1978 she began creating art quilts professionally. A few years later she picked up the threads of her early interest in architecture and began incorporating architectural themes in her quilts.

Most of her quilts now have to do with buildings, but even her "non-architectural pieces are often about grids and space." She has studied

Amphora II, 1993. 43 x 90 in. Photo by John Brennan.

architecture from an art history standpoint but has chosen not to study formal architectural drawing. After all, she says, "my buildings don't have to stand up." She prefers to create fantastic structures that are subject less to the rules of draftsmanship than to the dictates of her curiosity and imagination.

NINE OF HEARTS

"Calling All Hearts." Hand and machine piecing, appliqué and quilting. Cotton, rayon, cotton/polyester batting.

Susan Shie and James Acord

WOOSTER, OHIO

Born 1950, 1953

The Joker is an American contribution to the card deck, so it is appropriate that the Joker created by **Susan Shie** and **James Acord** is a shape shifter, that figure from Native American teachings who can change from one body to another as needed. Like the Joker who can take the identity of any card in the deck, the shape shifter can turn into any creature he pleases in order to fly, swim, run faster or become a guardian. This Joker is a trickster with a positive image, a shaman who creates illusions in order to heal theatrically.

Shie and Acord see themselves as "art shamans," working within the concept of "artist as healer." This Joker is a collaboration in which the two artists have each contributed their individual talents. Shie designed the piece—drawing with a laundry marker on white cotton and then painting with fabric paint—and did much of the embellishment, including her characteristic large hand-quilting stitches in bright embroidery floss. Acord created the leather hand appliqués that punctuate the border. Their Joker is a joint meditation, a "Green Quilt" that "affirms and celebrates the shaman within all of us." It is a vehicle for holistic healing and contains many symbols of intuition and magic: moons, sculls, hands and eyes. The frogs represent cleansing, and the Fimo clay crocodiles act as protectors through their strong Earth-connected magic spirits. Like a magician, the Joker

is juggling the suitmarks, and around him are the trickster's symbols of coyote and monkey.

Shie came to the art world formally, studying painting in college and earning an M.F.A. from the Kent State School of Art. She had learned to sew as a child and soon gravitated to quilts as her art form. Her subject matter has often been adventures from her daily life, portrayed in bright colors with her own invented symbolism and elaborately embellished with beads and other objects. She has been influenced in the nature of her artwork by her limited vision, having been legally blind since birth. "Everything I do depends on touch and closeness." She has concentrated on very tactile craft processes, such as ceramics and mixed media quilts, and tries to make her work accessible to the visually impaired.

Acord came to art quilts by way of his trade. He originally worked as a welder but admired leatherwork greatly and began using the company's machine shop to create leatherworking tools. He first produced functional leather goods for himself and his friends, but as his skill and his client list increased, he quit his welding job and opened a leather shop. When he shared studio space with Shie, she taught him sewing skills so that he could make leather clothing, and he soon began to explore leather as an art form. Even before the two married he had started collaborating with her on her quilts by creating

Tattle Tales—Crocodiles for Alzheimer's (detail), 1993. Courtesy of Mobilia Gallery, Cambridge, Massachusetts.

leather embellishments for added tactile quality. He also frequently adds details through airbrushing and free-hand machine embroidery—techniques that are difficult for Shie because of her eyesight and dependence on touch, but not for Acord, who became adept at precise mechanical control during his years as a welder.

The two artists complement each other and now always teach together. Their life together is a collaboration. They feel compelled to "say something useful" and have become leaders in the movement to make artworks vessels of healing, affirmation and ecological awareness. With this goal in mind, Shie founded the Green Quilts Project in 1989, a grassroots effort through which quilt artists spread beauty in the world and affirm their faith that the earth will be healed and nature's perfect balance recovered. The first quilt on which Shie and Acord collaborated was also the first Green Quilt ever made, "Back to Eden."

J O K E R

"Shape Shifter." Whole cloth with hand painting, embroidery, quilting, beading and embellishment. Cotton, satin, embroidery floss, tooled leather, beads, hand-formed polymer clay objects, decorative metal shapes, polyester batting.

jeN ShurtLiff

FARMINGTON, UTAH

Born 1957

Jen Shurtliff feels she has been an artist since before she can remember. When it came time for college she focused on fiber for her B.F.A. degree, and for her M.F.A. she studied painting. Afterward she built her career working in both mediums, sewing quilts with fabric and painting pictures on paper. The two art forms were always separate activities for her, mostly because of the very different approaches required for each medium. Traditional-style quilts are usually planned out carefully, and work on them proceeds very methodically and slowly, with the soft fabric being handled and manipulated constantly. Painting, on the other hand, is a spontaneous, direct process, but the painter works on a hard, rigid surface and stays a brush-length away from the work.

Shurtliff often wished that she could combine the close, tactile properties of quilting with the spontaneity of painting but found herself intimidated by "the preciousness of the fabric." She could not bring herself to paint free-form images on materials that she was used to working with so carefully and precisely. In 1988 she tried bridging the gap by painting on paper, tearing out the parts she liked and stitching them together into a quilt. After this she felt ready to take the step of actually painting on fabric. Now, in her quilts, she uses mostly fabrics that she has hand painted. She particularly enjoys airbrushing, a very spontaneous and direct process with distinctive effects that are achieved by physically manipulating the fabric painting surface.

For her Six of Clubs, Shurtliff chose to paint her vision of the card on whole cloth. Her six Club suitmarks are mosaic designs in a tile floor that looks real enough to walk on. She created the individual tiles by ripping freezer paper into small pieces and then positioning them on the cotton background and ironing them in place. She then airbrushed the quilt's surface with either red or black fabric paint to suggest the grout between the tiles. The freezer paper shapes acted as resists, leaving white tile shapes when they were removed, and she painted some of them with a brush in shades of gray and tan. For the card's design she decided to take a literal approach; to stay close to the standard playing card colors of red, white and black and to concentrate on the technical aspects. "Small pieces need to carry a lot of energy in them."

Shurtliff has titled her Six of Clubs "Shattered Beginnings" because it is subtly about order and disorder. The Club figures can be seen as three views of a man and a woman, Mr. and Mrs. Club. At the top of the card they are both surrounded by neatly concentric curves of tiles. In the middle the tiles around Mrs. Club begin to be less ordered, and at the bottom they are in complete chaos and are starting to disturb the orderly tiles around Mr. Club. "In reality we aren't as perfect as we seem."

The subjects of many of Shurtliff's quilts reflect her own life and concerns, and she sees art as an effective catalyst for initiating dialog on important issues. Lately she has been working a lot with her dreams. She thinks that trying to explain why she made a quilt the way she did or what it means is like trying to explain what your dreams are about. "I've given up on the idea that I'm in control of my artwork; I just watch it unfold."

SIX OF CLUBS

"Shattered Beginnings." Whole cloth with airbrushing, hand painting, machine quilting. Cotton, cotton batting.

LYNNE SWARD

VIRGINIA BEACH, VIRGINIA

Born 1938

"Life is too fast. I'd like for people to slow down and really study my things, to take some time with them. This is my way of entertaining the public," says **Lynne Sward**. Her complex quilts are intricate constructions of a myriad of tiny elements. She delineates larger shapes by varying the colors or character of the many minuscule components but maintains her favorite effect of pattern on pattern, which holds continuing surprises for the viewer.

For her playing card, Sward represented the Queen of Diamonds with a giant initial Q. She created the main image with mostly black fabrics and decorated it with photo transfers of spectacular diamonds and of Elizabeth Taylor (whom Sward thought of immediately as a "queen of diamonds") in the role of Queen Cleopatra. The center of the Q suggests the faceted surface of a solitaire diamond, sprinkled with rhinestones and crystals for added glitter. Jewel-tone fabrics radiate out from the Q and are embellished by photo transfers of postage stamps portraying Queen Elizabeth I and II and queen bees. Sward also included other commercial fabrics that are printed with crowns, diamond shapes and more bees.

For construction of the Queen of Diamonds, Sward used her favorite technique of "scatter and sew," which she describes as "a joyful unencumbered experience." She began by applying a fusible web backing to a selection of fabrics and then cutting them into small triangles to reflect a diamond's angular shape. She then "scattered" the triangles over a ground cloth according to her design and ironed the pieces in place. She had the photo transfer images made on a laser printer at a copy graphics store, trimmed the resulting fabric pictures to the desired shapes and hand appliquéd them to the quilt's surface. When she was satisfied with the final arrangement of all her pieces, she secured everything with free-hand machine embroidery that also served as the quilting.

Sward prefers to work with commercial fabrics instead of painting or dyeing her own. She likes to discover "weird and unique fabrics," and when she does she buys minimal amounts in every colorway produced, filing them in her studio storage bins according to type rather than color. She loves to put many different materials together, trying always to make them work "in a fine art way," as if her tiny fabric pieces were brush strokes.

Sward's art education began with classes at the Art Institute of Chicago when she was young, and she went on to study advertising art in college. She had always been "obsessed with making things" and became interested in quilting after seeing a quilt exhibit at the Art Institute in the mid 1970s. However, she was attracted to the idea of working quilt-style in three dimensions instead of two. She explored soft sculpture in the form of art pieces, dolls and jewelry and finally made her first flat quilt in 1982. Since then she has alternated between two and three dimensions. Sward considers the quilted clothing and jewelry that she still makes to be basically a commercial venture, but she emphasizes that she makes her art quilts to please herself and to have fun. "I have to have fun. I'd rather let other people handle deep issues. I like humor; we need it to exist."

QUEEN OF DIAMONDS

"Queens and Diamonds." Photo transfer, machine appliqué and free-motion embroidery, hand stitching.
Cotton, cotton blend fabrics, crystal and plastic cabochons, flannel batting.

MicHeLe VerNoN

F A L L S   C H U R C H ,   V I R G I N I A
....
Born 1951

Technically, **Michele Vernon's** Ace of Diamonds is a very simple quilt. She uses one of the oldest and easiest construction methods: piecing together rectangular fabric blocks of the same size. She has not embellished it in any way, and her quilting is the straightforward "in the ditch" technique of sewing along the seams that join the blocks. The structure is traditional and ordered. However, her subtle placement of color and attention to line produce a striking and sophisticated design that commands respect for this powerful playing card.

Vernon's Ace of Diamonds has a definite cubist character. The fractured edges of the central Diamond figure shift in and out at random, and the shading of various blocks sometimes suggests superimposed rectangular patterns. The only variation on her basic rectangular block is an occasional diagonal division into triangles, but this simple modification is enough to define the hard-edged sharpness of the Diamond's angles, repeating them down to the figure's core and echoing them outside its borders. The multiple reflected images give this playing card Diamond the faceted brilliance of a precious stone. The shadow of a Diamond, or perhaps of the letter A, acts as the traditional corner index that confirms a playing card's identity.

The Ace of Diamonds was Vernon's immediate choice to interpret, partly because her nickname at home is "Ace," but mostly because the card's simplicity and straightforward geometric nature related to recent artwork that she had been doing. For the last several years her quilts have had architectural themes or have been interpretations of maps. The clean lines of architectural elements attract Vernon, as do the navigational nature of maps and the precision of their grids. "I always have to know where I am." She was influenced by the color of old maps in her choice of fabrics for the background of her card.

Vernon's career as an art quilter has evolved through a series of responses. Her bachelor of arts in history qualified her for a job with the Smithsonian Institution, and after two years of being surrounded by art she was inspired to return to school and study design. She chose North Carolina State University, partially because its School of Design had associations with the University's textile department and she had always enjoyed working with textiles. While there she also found herself influenced, through proximity, by the architectural curriculum. Several years later, after working as a graphic designer creating logos and brochures, she started making quilts for babies and as gifts when suddenly she realized that she could combine her love of fabric and her graphics training in the medium of quilting. Quilting also allowed her a more consistently colorful way of working than did commercial art,

City Vision, 1991. 48 x 48 in. View of the District of Columbia; part of a series inspired by maps.

where color is expensive. Vernon was immediately drawn by publicity for the National Trust for Historic Preservation's second annual "Tactile Architecture" show in 1988, and she realized that this was a direction she wanted her work to take. Her architecturally inspired art quilts have been accepted regularly into this national juried show every year since.

ACE OF DIAMONDS

Machine piecing and quilting. Cotton, cotton blend fabrics, painted canvas, polyester fleece batting.

jeanne WilLiamson

NATICK, MASSACHUSETTS

Born 1957

Jeanne Williamson's Two of Clubs is the product of both simple technique and advanced technology. An early career teaching art to the physically and mentally disabled honed her expertise in stamping designs on fabric with hand-cut rubber erasers. A later job designing fonts and icons for a desktop publishing company caused her to start seeing everything in terms of "pixels," the smallest addressable elements in digital computer imagery, and helped her to become very comfortable working within a grid system. The combined result has been her series of stamp-art quilts that resemble the pointillist images on the screen of a color monitor.

In her quilts she has not tried to duplicate computer images; she has merely borrowed the digital principle of using a basic design unit to build shapes. On her Two of Clubs, the one-inch squares that make up the quilt's basic grid might be considered her pixels, but she has taken an artist's liberty in sometimes using only a half or a quarter of each pixel or filling the square space with a circle. She also has added a second layer of pixels at each intersection of the original grid.

In the first stamped layer, Williamson builds images of the black Club suitmarks and corner indices in the classic playing card arrangement against a background of purple, green and blue. The second layer adds alternating diagonal rows of red circles and orange and yellow squares. "I couldn't decide which colors to use so I used them all." The combination of colors of the two layers of stamps produces still a third color group. Because of the strict symmetrical arrangement she sought, the stamping process needed to be very precise, with no room for error. In order to ensure that a sufficient amount of color was transferred with each impression, she painted the surface of the stamp with a brush each time she used it. After the stamping process was complete, she washed the cloth in order to blend the color evenly and to soften the fabric. She then machine quilted along the lines of the basic grid and along some of the diagonal lines created by the second grid.

The final effect of Williamson's Two of Clubs suggests several associations to the viewer. The symmetry and geometric patterning of Islamic tile work quickly come to mind. The bright colors and simple patterns of Amish quilts have influenced some of her other pieces and are suggested by this quilt, particularly with the contrast of the black Clubs. The pattern-within-a-pattern effect of the uniform design units and subtle layers of color suggest the hidden shapes in a color blindness test, or perhaps a marked deck of cards with face values visible on their backs—but only to the card shark wearing a special pair of glasses.

Garden in Front of the Lattice, 1994. 45 x 43 in. Photo by David Caras.

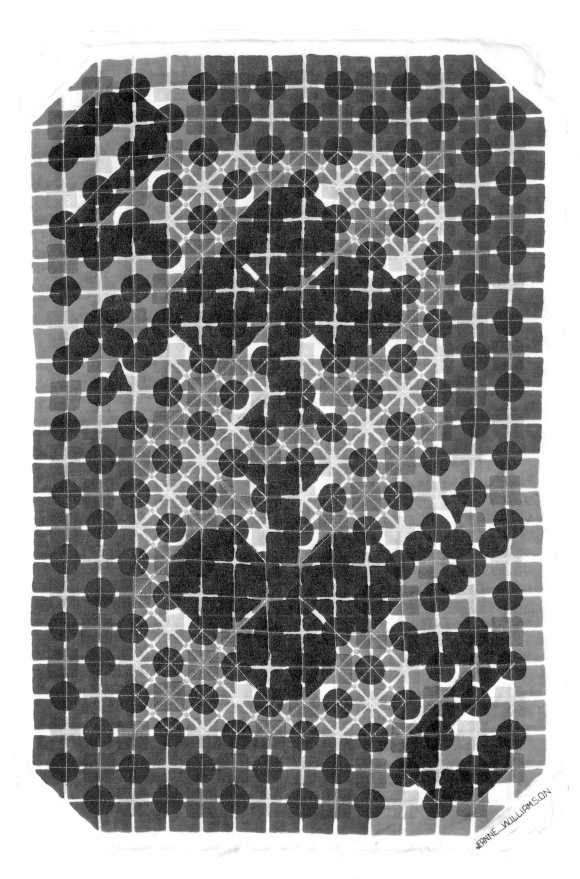

TWO OF CLUBS
Whole cloth with hand stamping, machine quilting. Cotton, fabric paint, polyester batting.

selected bibliography

ART QUILTS

Many books have been published recently on the subject of quilts and quilt making, but most concern themselves with instruction and provide patterns. The publications listed here are among the few that document or discuss the art quilt movement. Included are a number of catalogs from important exhibits and several thoughtful articles on the state of art quilts.

The Artist and the Quilt. Charlotte Robinson, editor. New York: Alfred A. Knopf, 1983.

Chase, Patti. *The Contemporary Quilt: New American Quilts and Fabric Art.* New York: E. P. Dutton, 1978.

The FIBERARTS Design Book. New York: Hastings House Publishers, 1980.

The FIBERARTS Design Book II. Asheville, N.C.: Lark Books, 1983.

FIBERARTS Design Book Three. Kate Mathews, editor. Asheville, N.C:. Lark Books, 1987.

FIBERARTS Design Book Four. Nancy Orban, editor. Asheville, N.C.: Lark Books, 1991.

Fiber Expressions: The Contemporary Quilt. Exhibition catalog, Quilt National '87. West Chester, Pa.: Schiffer Publishing, Ltd., 1987.

Holstein, Jonathan. *The Pieced Quilt: An American Design Tradition.* Greenwich, Conn.: New York Graphic Society, Ltd., 1973.

James, Michael. "Beyond Tradition: The Art of the Studio Quilt." *American Craft*, Feb/Mar 1985.

Jessen, Carol. "Contemporary Quilts: Moving beyond the Art vs. Craft Debate." *Surface Design Journal*, Fall 1991.

Lavitt, Wendy. *Contemporary Pictorial Quilts.* Layton, Utah: Gibbs Smith, 1993.

McMorris, Penny and Michael Kile. *The Art Quilt.* San Francisco: Quilt Digest Press, 1986.

The New Quilt 1. Exhibition catalog, Quilt National '91. Newtown, Conn.: Taunton Press, 1991.

The New Quilt 2. Exhibition catalog, Quilt National '93. Newtown, Conn.: Taunton Press, 1993.

New Quilts: Interpretations & Innovations. Exhibition catalog, Quilt National '89. West Chester, Pa.: Schiffer Publishing, Ltd., 1989.

The Quilt: New Directions for an American Tradition. Exhibition catalog, Quilt National '83. West Chester, Pa.: Schiffer Publishing Ltd., 1983.

Quilts: The State of an Art. Exhibition catalog, Quilt National '85. West Chester, Pa.: Schiffer Publishing, Ltd., 1985.

Smith, Barbara Lee. *Celebrating the Stitch.* Newton, Conn.: Taunton Press, 1991.

The Quiltmaker's Art: Contemporary Quilts and their Makers. Joanne Mattera, editor. Asheville, N.C.: Lark Books, 1982.

Visions: The Art of the Quilt. Deborah Timby, editor. Exhibition catalog, Quilt San Diego '92. Lafayette, Calif.: C&T Publishing, 1992.

Visions: Layers of Excellence. Stevii Thompson Graves, editor. Exhibition catalog, Quilt San Diego '94. Lafayette, Calif.: C&T Publishing, 1994.

Visions: Quilts of a New Decade. Exhibition catalog, Quilt San Diego '90. Lafayette, Calif.: C&T Publishing, Ltd., 1990.

PLAYING CARDS

Beal, George. *Playing Cards and Their Story.* Newton Abbot, England: David & Charles, 1975.

Field, Albert. *Transformation Playing Cards.* Stamford, Conn.: U.S. Games Systems, Inc., 1987.

Hutton, Alice. *The Cards Can't Lie: Prophetic, Educational & Playing Cards.* London: Jupiter Books, 1979.

Mann, Sylvia. *Collecting English Playing Cards.* London: Stanley Gibbons Publications, Ltd., 1978.

Tilley, Roger. *Playing Cards.* London: Octopus Books, 1973.